Improve Your Tennis IQ

Improve Your Tennis IQ

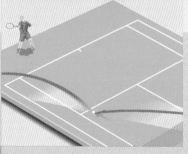

Charles Applewhaite

Illustrations
by Richard Burgess
and Andrew Green

All inquiries should be addressed to:
Barron's Educational Series, Inc.
250 Wireless Boulevard
Hauppauge, New York 11788
http://www.barronseduc.com

Library of Congress Catalog Card Number 2002101222

ISBN 0–7641–2257–6

QUAR.IYT

Conceived, designed, and produced by
Quarto Publishing plc
The Old Brewery
6 Blundell Street
London N7 9BH

Project Editors Tracie Lee Davis, Fiona Robertson
Art Editor Jill Mumford
Text Editor Andrew Armitage
Designer Karin Skånberg
Photographer Ian Howes
Illustrators Richard Burgess and Andrew Green
Proofreader Anne Plume
Indexer Diana Le Core

Art Director Moira Clinch
Publisher Piers Spence

Manufactured by Pica Digital Pte Ltd, Singapore
Printed in Singapore by Star Standard Industries Pte Ltd

9 8 7 6 5 4 3 2 1

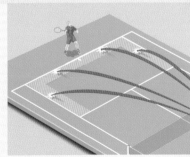

Contents

Introduction

Tennis is a wonderful game for all ages and abilities. The beauty of tennis is that it can be enjoyed by a huge range of players. Whether you are a social player who plays simply to meet your friends or a motivated keep-fit enthusiast, whether you are a beginner just starting to learn the game or an accomplished match player, tennis can offer what you are looking for and much more besides.

I believe that developing a better understanding of strategy and tactics will give any tennis player a basis for self-improvement. But how can you manage this? Try the following simple and organized route to better tennis:

1. Develop an understanding of a particular tactic or technique.
2. Identify your own strengths and weaknesses in this area.
3. Evaluate your performance against a reasonable standard (from beginner to high performance).
4. Set up a training routine to enhance your performance.
5. Set yourself realistic small goals for improvement.
6. "Don't think about it—do it!"
7. Enjoy the challenge.

I hope this book will stimulate your self-analysis and self-improvement. Finally, one last thought: Tennis is very much a personal game. When you watch the top players in competition you see how diverse are the ways in which they play. Try to approach the game in a manner that reflects your personality. There is no one way to play, only certain basic principles you will need to follow if you want to play well or to improve. Read the solutions to the tennis problems, but remember that there is always a place in tennis for the unexpected or the unorthodox.

Have fun improvising!

Charles Applewhaite

How to use this book

This book is aimed toward all standards of player, from beginner through tournament competitor. It is designed to set you thinking about certain aspects of tennis by posing the questions that are frequently asked of coaches, and then encouraging you to choose your own answers. When you have picked an answer you should turn over the page and check whether it is the appropriate technique or tactic. Choosing an answer yourself will relate the solution to your own game, and this process will help you to become a better player.

The focus of the book is mainly on the tactics and techniques of tennis—on the "What to do" and the "How to do it." The strategy of the game has been divided into four areas of play that cover all situations in tennis: The serve; returning serve; when both players are at the back, and net play. Some techniques of physical fitness and mental approach are also covered, by posing basic questions that are often asked by players. However, there is only a taster of these two important subjects, which each deserves a book in its own right.

Each question about a particular technique or tactic is accompanied by a selection of possible answers (some correct and some incorrect)

Illustrations show players demonstrating different techniques

The next pages give correct answers to the questions, and explain why each answer is the best solution

Key shows the color coding of "players" and "opponents"

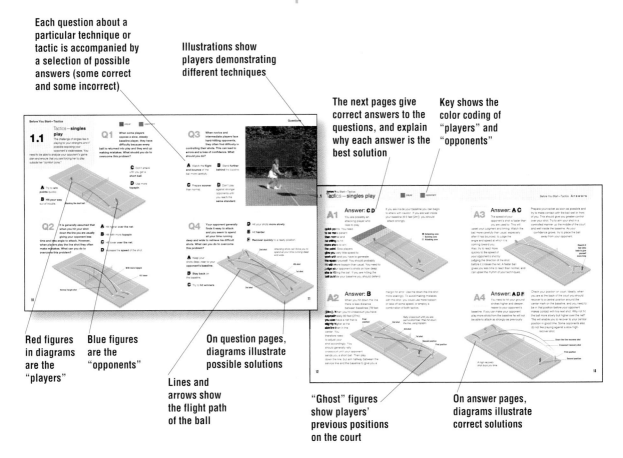

Red figures in diagrams are the "players"

Blue figures are the "opponents"

On question pages, diagrams illustrate possible solutions

Lines and arrows show the flight path of the ball

"Ghost" figures show players' previous positions on the court

On answer pages, diagrams illustrate correct solutions

Tactics

1

In the battles of tennis as in war, it is not always the biggest and strongest who win. Very often it is the smartest tactician who finds an opponent's weakness and wins the points, sets, and matches. You need to evaluate your own and your partner's strengths and weaknesses and make a personal game plan. Be flexible and adapt your game plan during the match, and enforce it on your opponent. Remember the saying "If you fail to prepare, prepare to fail!"

player   *opponent*

Tactics—**singles play**

1.1

The challenge of singles lies in playing to your strengths and if possible exposing your opponent's weaknesses. You need to be able to analyze your opponent's game plan and ensure that you are forcing her to play outside her "comfort zone."

Q1 When some players oppose a slow, steady baseline player, they have difficulty because every ball is returned into play and they end up making mistakes. What should you do to overcome this problem?

C Don't attack until you get a **short ball**.

D Use more **topspin**.

A Try to **win points** quickly.

B **Hit your way** out of trouble.

Attacking the short ball

Q2 It is generally assumed that when you hit your shot down the line you are usually giving your opponent less time and less angle to attack. However, when players play the line shot they often make mistakes. What can you do to overcome this problem?

A Hit higher **over the net**.

B Hit with more **topspin**.

C Hit lower **over the net**.

D Increase the **speed** of the shot.

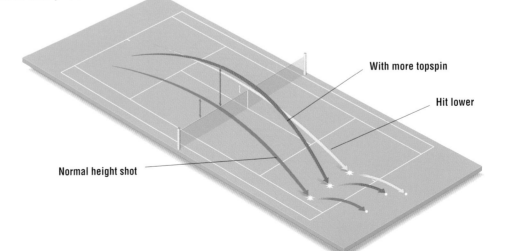

With more topspin

Hit lower

Normal height shot

Q3

When novice and intermediate players face hard-hitting opponents, they often find difficulty in controlling their shots. This can lead to errors and a loss of confidence. What should you do?

A Watch the **flight and bounce** of the ball more carefully.

B Stand **further behind** the baseline.

C Prepare **sooner** than normal.

D Don't play against stronger opponents until you reach the **same standard**.

Q4

Your opponent generally finds it easy to attack and you seem to spend all your time running deep and wide to retrieve his difficult shots. What can you do to overcome this problem?

A Keep your shots deep, near to your **opponent's baseline.**

B **Stay back** on the baseline.

C Try to **hit winners**.

D Hit your shots **more slowly**.

E Hit **harder**.

F **Recover quickly** to a ready position.

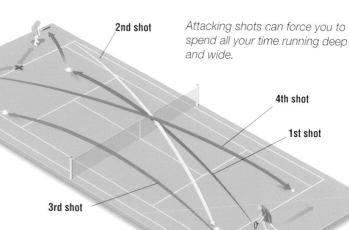

2nd shot

Attacking shots can force you to spend all your time running deep and wide.

4th shot

1st shot

3rd shot

1.1 Tactics—**singles play**

■ player   ■ opponent

A1 **Answer: C D**

You are possibly an attacking player who likes to play quick points. You need to be more patient than normal and be willing to hit more shots to win the point. Slow players give you very little speed to work with and you have to generate the speed yourself. You should probably hit with more topspin than usual. You need to judge your opponent's shots on how deep she is hitting the ball. If you are hitting the ball outside your baseline you should defend.

If you are inside your baseline you can begin to attack with caution. If you are well inside your baseline (6.5 feet [2m]), you should attack strongly.

■ Defending zone
□ Building zone
■ Attacking zone

A2 **Answer: B**

When you hit down the line there is less distance between baselines (78 feet [24m]). When you hit crosscourt you have approximately 90 feet (27m); you also have a net that is slightly higher at the sideline than in the center. You therefore need to adjust your shot accordingly. You should generally rally crosscourt until your opponent sends you a short ball. Then play down the line, but aim halfway between the service line and the baseline to give you a

margin for error. Use the down-the-line shot more sparingly. To avoid making mistakes with this shot, you could use more topspin or take off some speed, or employ a combination of both tactics.

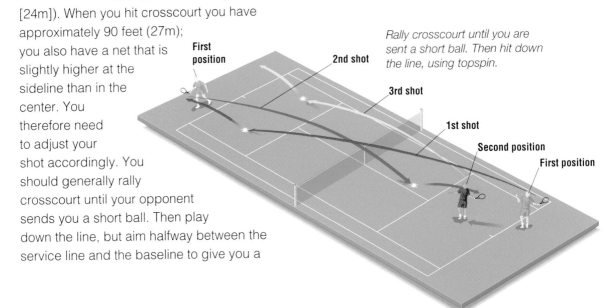

Rally crosscourt until you are sent a short ball. Then hit down the line, using topspin.

First position

2nd shot

3rd shot

1st shot

Second position

First position

A3 **Answer: A C**

The speed of your opponent's shot is faster than you are used to. This will upset your judgment and timing. Watch the ball more carefully than usual, especially after it has bounced, to judge the angle and speed at which it is coming toward you. Also, try to react more quickly to the speed of your opponent's shot by judging the direction of the shot before it crosses the net. A faster ball gives you less time to react than normal, and can upset the rhythm of your

techniques. Prepare your racket as soon as possible and try to make contact with the ball well in front of you. This should give you greater control over your shot. Try to aim your shot in a controlled manner up the middle of the court and well inside the baseline. As your confidence grows, try to place the ball away from your opponent.

Stand 6.5 feet (2m) back to give yourself more time

A4 **Answer: A D F**

You need to hit your ground strokes higher and deeper, nearer to your opponent's baseline. If you can make your opponent play more shots from the baseline he will not be able to attack as strongly as previously.

Check your position on court. Ideally, when you are at the back of the court you should recover to a central position around the center mark on the baseline, and you need to be in that position before your opponent makes contact with his next shot. Why not hit the ball more slowly but higher over the net? This will enable you to recover to your central position in good time. Some opponents also do not like playing against a slow high-recovery shot.

Down-the-line recovery shot

Crosscourt recovery shot

First position

Second position

A high recovery shot buys you time.

13

■ *player*　　■ *opponent*

Tactics—**doubles play**

1.2

Many players like doubles because they enjoy playing as a team, sharing responsibilities and successes. Remember to support each other whether you are winning or losing. You should have a previously agreed game plan to follow, although you may need to adapt it during the match.

Q5 **Many novice tennis players feel uncomfortable at the net when their partner is serving. They are unsure of which shot to take, and can end up hiding away in the sidelines taking little part in the point. In that situation, what should you do?**

A **Go back** to the baseline.

B Move **closer** to the sidelines.

C **Be positive** and go for anything near you.

D Try to **cover your half** of the court.

Partner moved back to baseline

Partner moved closer to sidelines

Q6 **Both you and your partner appear to have a problem deciding who plays a ball coming down the middle. You have already crashed rackets three times and now you have each left the ball for the other—with disastrous results! Is there anything you can do to decide who plays a ball coming down the middle?**

C The **younger** player.

D Both players **should agree** before the match.

E The player **nearer to the ball**.

A The **backhand** court player.

B The **forehand** court player.

Q7

My partner is at the net and I am at the back of the court and my opponents send a deep lob over my partner. Who should take the shot?

A My **partner**.

B I should **run across** and play the shot.

C **Both partners** should go for the ball.

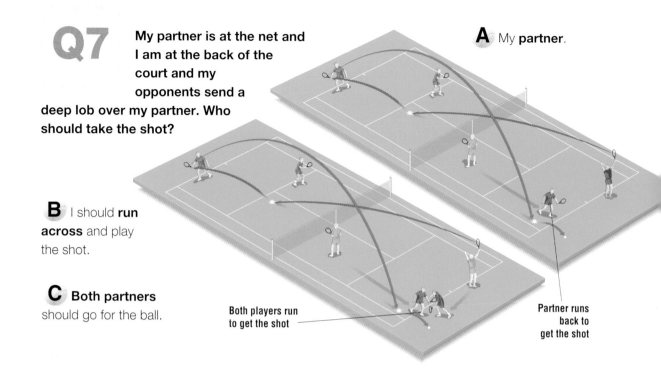

Both players run to get the shot

Partner runs back to get the shot

Q8

When players return serve in doubles they may find difficulty because they have only half a court to aim toward, since the server's partner is covering the other half. In singles the court is 27 feet (8.2m) wide and in doubles 36 feet (11m) wide. However, with the partner covering half the court the returner is left with a target area of only 18 feet (5.5m) wide. What can he do to develop consistency on the return of serve?

A Carefully place the ball **back into play**.

C Go for **attacking** shots.

D Be consistent; hit at a **speed you can control** to your target area.

E As a variation, **lob** the net player.

Stand 6.5 feet (2m) back to receive serve

Hit the ball carefully to land near the sideline and 6.5 feet (2m) inside the baseline

B Stand well back to **receive**.

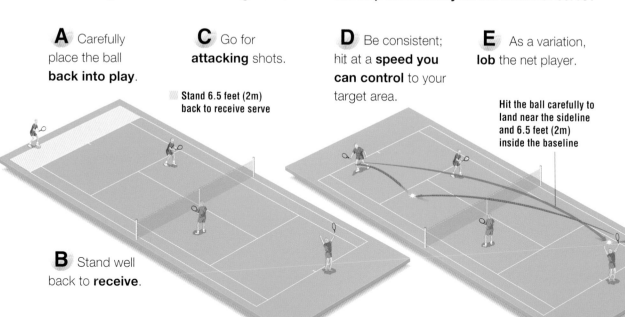

■ player   ■ opponent

A5 Answer: C D

Whatever level you are at as a player, your position at the net is crucial in helping to win your partner's service game. The first point to consider is that your position at the net generally forces your opponent to return crosscourt into a smaller area (half a doubles court), which can lead to errors on the return. The second point to remember is that mistakes are part of the process of learning, so don't worry. As a novice player, able to hit a basic volley, you can begin to enjoy net play. Try to play any ball that is close to you or will land in your side of the court. If you are an intermediate or improver, now is the time to make your presence felt by trying to intercept a weak crosscourt return. Even if you make a mistake, on subsequent returns your opponents will be distracted by you and may start to make errors themselves.

▨ **Area to cover for intermediate net player**
▦ **Area to cover for novice net player**

A6 Answer: D E

Many players can find the transition from singles to doubles play very exciting and stimulating. It can be great fun trying to build a doubles partnership into an effective team. Some players, however, find doubles play creates conflict and confusion as to who plays which shots and when. The first rule to remember is that there are not any hard and fast rules, except on the serve and return of serve. What you need to do is set your own ground rules as to who plays what—and when. You will find after a few matches together that you and your partner start to fit in with each other and "read" each other's positioning. You will also find that your discussions during and after each match will clarify some issues. Three general principles are worth noting in the situation of a ball down the middle:

1. Never let the ball go between both players; it is better for both to go for it rather than both leave it.

2. If you have time, let the player with the stronger shot play the ball.

3. The player nearer the net should always try to play it first.

A winning shot, left by both both opponents.

A7

Answer: B

In top-level tennis the player at the net will almost always play her own lob with a smash (generally for a winner). If the net player is poor at smashing or too slow going backwards she should call "yours" in good time to her partner, who can then run across the baseline to cover her half of the court. The net player should now move across to cover her partner's half of the court. Generally she should join her partner at the baseline in a defensive position. However, if the lob is short, the net player should always play it.

Partner moves across to cover

Server moves across to take lob

A8

Answer: D E

The comparison of return of serve in singles and doubles throws up some interesting tactical principles. In singles there are more possibilities as to where you can safely return the ball. However, in doubles your opponent net player restricts your options considerably. You therefore have less court to aim for and you will need to be more disciplined in where you hit the ball. The main objectives are to put the return in play and keep it away from the player at the net while making the return as difficult as possible for the server. If the server stays back you should aim your return to hit the inside sideline and land approximately 6–7 feet (2m) inside the baseline. If you are playing against a serve volleyer you should aim to land your return on their service line to force them to play a difficult low volley. Both these returns should force your opponent on the defensive.

▓ **Playing against serve and stay back**
▒ **Playing against serve and volley**

Width of half a doubles court
Width of doubles court
Width of singles court

The Serve

2 The serve can be the most rewarding shot in tennis— and for some, the most frustrating. It is the only time when you are in complete control of the game. You have the ball in your hand and your opponent is not making you run or forcing you into difficult situations. The success of your serve is entirely up to you! An efficient serving action requires technical skill and coordination, but tactical common sense is also needed to maximize your advantage. You should be able to use your serve as an attacking weapon by varying speed, direction, and spin. Controlled aggression is the key to serving success.

2.1

Basic techniques

Many players experience difficulty with the serve when they first start playing. They often have problems in coordinating the ball toss and the hitting action, and consequently lose accuracy and power. If you can develop the basic fundamentals when you first start playing, it will pay dividends later.

Q2

It can be quite tricky to coordinate both hands when you are serving. How can you toss the ball both accurately and at the right time to achieve a smooth hit?

A Start with **both hands together** away from the body.

Q1

You are not sure how to stand at the start of your serve. When you watch top players in action you see many different starting positions and it looks a little confusing. So how should a player who has just started playing position himself before he begins to serve?

A **Sideways** to the opponent.

B Bring **both hands down** together to the side of the body.

C Release the ball in the air when your ball hand is **level with your head**.

B **Closed** stance to the opponent.

D Release the ball in the air when your ball hand is **level with your chest**.

C **Open** stance to the opponent.

Q3 The ball toss on the serve is the only time in tennis when you are totally in control of the ball. You can throw it almost anywhere you want to enable you to hit a good (basic) serve. So where should you place it?

Ball height when thrown

Ball position when hit

A At a height level with the **top of your racket** when you are fully stretched.

B Slightly **in front and to the side** of your body, near the front foot.

C Slightly **behind your head** and over your left shoulder.

Q4 Many novice players and even experienced players can find the throwing action on the serve quite difficult and not comfortable. What can you do to overcome this problem and develop a more coordinated throwing action?

A Try to **gain rhythm** by working both hands together.

B Try to **strengthen your shoulder muscles** and tense them on contact.

C Try to use **more wrist action**.

D Practice throwing **overarm** with various lightweight balls.

E Keep your throwing wrist **rigid**.

Answer: A

This is the best starting position for a novice player to stand in when about to serve. In singles you need to stand close to the center mark so you can cover any return of serve to your forehand or backhand side equally well. A sideways position when you serve will help the transfer of your body momentum toward the direction in which you are aiming. If you draw an imaginary line from the end of your feet, this line should point to the middle of the opponent's service box. It is a similar starting position to when you are throwing a ball at a target. If you have a closed stance (B), you will tend to rotate the body prior to the hit, which can generate slice on the ball. If you have an open stance (C), you will find it difficult to gain racket and body momentum toward your target area.

Standing sideways to your opponent will help you serve with more accuracy.

Serving to forehand court

Serving to backhand court

Answer: A B D

When you are serving it is the only time you have complete control over the situation. The ball is in your hand and you can place it in the air and hit it as you wish. This is the time when you need to coordinate a regular movement pattern with both hands working together. This should then lead into an effective serving action.

Release the ball when the hand is at chest height and the racket hand is at hip height.

1. Both hands should start together, pointing toward the opponent. The hand holding the ball should be resting lightly against the racket frame or strings.
2. The two hands should move downward together almost to the side of the body.
3. The ball hand should begin to move upward, with the ball gently resting in the palm of the hand.
4. The racket hand should continue downward and separate from the ball hand.
5. The ball should be released (placed in the air) when the hand is at approximately chest height. At this time the racket hand should be at about hip height.

Answer: A B

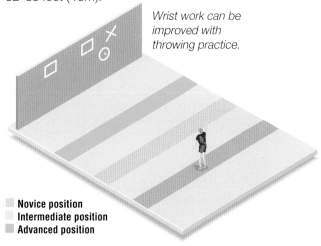

An effective and accurate ball toss is the key to consistent serving. If you can throw the ball in the air in the right place and at the right time, the basic serve can become a strong feature of your game. The height of the ball toss should be consistent and reach approximately to the top of your racket when held above the head. It is easier to hit the ball when it has reached its apex and is just beginning to fall, because at this point the ball is almost stationary in the air. You need the ball toss to be placed forward of your front shoulder, slightly in front of your body, to allow transfer of your body weight (momentum) into the shot and toward the direction of your hit. You need it on the racket side of your body to ensure that you are at full stretch at contact.

Throw the ball forward of your shoulder on your racket side, and hit the ball when it is at the top of the racket.

Answer: A C D

When you watch top-class servers in action they tend to develop power, speed, and accuracy with ease. However, it is difficult to pick out the skill in the throwing action because at this point in the serve the racket head is traveling so fast. If you can video their serve and play back the tape in slow motion, you will get a better picture of their skill in the final phase of the serve. You need to synchronize both hands during the action, which should lead into a good throwing position. The racket's head speed prior to contact is generated through a coordinated sequence of movements using various muscles and joints known as the *coordination chain*. Starting from the ground, each segment of the body should gradually build up its momentum until, just before contact, the wrist comes into play and accelerates the racket head to maximum speed. Develop wrist work on the serve by throwing a ball at a target on a wall from a distance of about 32–33 feet (10m).

Wrist work can be improved with throwing practice.

■ Novice position
▨ Intermediate position
■ Advanced position

2.2

Controlling, **directing,** and increasing **speed**

Top players seem capable of pinpoint accuracy on their serve while they are hitting at enormous speed. This must be the ultimate dream of every club player. What do we need to consider to improve in these areas?

Q6 The accuracy of the serve is a problem for many players. The first challenge is to hit the ball from over your head into an area of the court that is around 25 percent of your normal target area in baseline play. What do you need to do to direct the ball more accurately into a small area?

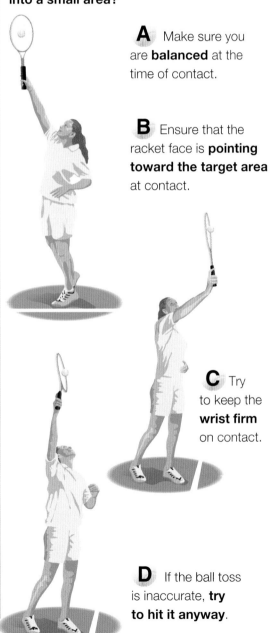

A Make sure you are **balanced** at the time of contact.

B Ensure that the racket face is **pointing toward the target area** at contact.

C Try to keep the **wrist firm** on contact.

D If the ball toss is inaccurate, **try to hit it anyway**.

Q5 The grip, or the way you hold the racket, is extremely important in developing the correct amount of control, power, and spin. Is there a difference between the grips held by the novice and the expert? Which of these service grips is most suitable for which player as a general principle?

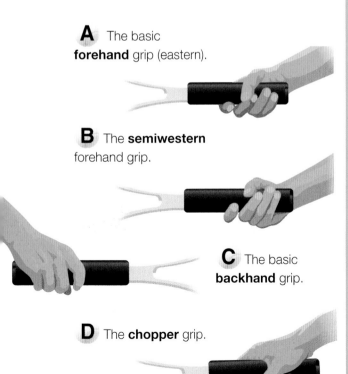

A The basic **forehand** grip (eastern).

B The **semiwestern** forehand grip.

C The basic **backhand** grip.

D The **chopper** grip.

A fast and powerful serve will often force the opponent to make an error on her return of serve. What can we do to generate speed on the serve to make it harder to return?

A Use the **legs** more at the start.

B Try to use all **body segments**.

C Keep your **body weight** static.

D Tighten your **arm and shoulder** just before contact.

Many players find there is little difference between their first and second serves—except for speed. As they develop their skills, they may introduce spin as a challenge to the player who is returning serve. What tactical points are important to remember for the player who has not yet mastered spin and wants to develop her consistency and confidence?

A Speed up your first serve by **increasing** the throwing action.

B **Slow down** the rhythm of the whole serve.

C Make sure that the racket face is pointing at contact **toward the target area**.

D Don't be too aggressive with power, but **think about accuracy** and placement.

A5

Answer: A D

The ideal grip for a player to use on the serve is the chopper grip. This will enable the player to serve with power and accuracy and use both topspin and slice as a variation of the basic flat serve. If you were able to master the chopper grip, you could expect to add a new dimension to your serving. Most novice players feel more comfortable holding the racket for the serve with a basic eastern forehand grip, commonly known as a "shake-hands" grip. This grip will feel strong and the player will probably find it easier to direct the ball to the target and get it into play. However, once the novice player with this starting grip has achieved a degree of safety and accuracy, it should be time to move toward the more efficient chopper grip. Players who want to progress their serving ability will need to develop more racket-head speed through effective wrist work, which can come only when they use the correct grip.

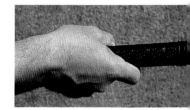

Chopper grip

"Shake-hands" grip

A6

Answer: A B

Good balance is the key to playing most shots in tennis effectively. If you can achieve a sound, balanced position with your body when you contact the ball, you should have the basis for a good serve. If you are off balance, your accuracy will be affected. You need to point the racket face, at contact with the ball, toward the target area to achieve accuracy. The ball is in contact with the strings for only three-thousandths of a second, so you need to get it right at the most important time (contact point). If you place a poor, inaccurate ball toss in the air, you will have little chance of retaining your balance and directing the ball into the service box. The rules state that you do not have to hit it and can stop the serve and try again. So be aware of your ball toss and take advantage of this helpful rule of tennis.

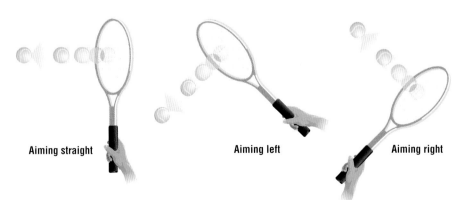

Aiming straight   **Aiming left**   **Aiming right**

Make sure the racket face is pointing toward the target area.

Answer: A B

A powerful serve comes from a buildup of speed that culminates in an explosive throwing action of the racket head at a ball that is in the right place to be hit. It requires rhythm, timing, coordination, balance, speed, and momentum to be in place at the appropriate stages of the serve. Power will always generate from the legs, which need to push against the ground to start the first stage of any powerful movement. Then it leads into the coordination chain, which comprises ankles, knees, hips, shoulders, elbows, and wrist. As each one of these segments is brought into play, there should be a gradual increase of power and speed, which culminates in a fast wrist action prior to ball contact. When you first start trying to generate speed on your serve, don't worry about getting the ball in the court. Try to log your speed and increase it by extra racket-head speed. Once you have developed this, the next stage is to develop control of your speed.

Generate power from your legs up through your body to create speed on your serve.

Answer: C D

When you are about to hit your first serve you are generally considered to be in an attacking position and your opponent is probably going to be in a more defensive position. On your second serve there is quite a role reversal; you now have to put the ball in play probably much more softly. The opponent is probably inside his baseline, looking to start an attack, and you feel on the defensive. This is where you need to ensure that you keep on the attack by observing the following:

1. Slow down your first serve a little and try to hit a high percentage (70 percent) of first serves into play in a controlled manner.
2. Pick a small target area in your opponent's service box and concentrate on directing the racket face, at contact, toward the target area.

Concentrate on small target areas. Here, the targets are approximately 5 x 6½ feet (1.5 x 2m).

▥ **Forehand court targeted**

2.3

Using **spin** for effect—**slice**

Almost all shots in tennis are hit with some form of spin (most balls are spinning or rotating as they cross the net). Although this is not advised for novices, it can be an added strength if you can spin the ball intentionally.

Q9 What are the tactical advantages of a slice serve, and which of the following answers would be correct for a right-handed player?

A In flight the ball will swing **from right to left.**

B After the bounce the ball will **straighten up.**

C After the bounce the ball will **continue to swing** from right to left.

D After the bounce the ball **will break from left to right.**

E The ball will **stay lower than normal** after the bounce.

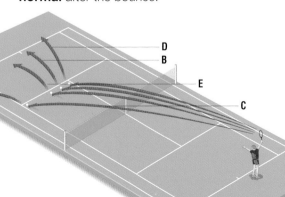

Q10 Can you use slice as a tactical advantage on both your first and second serves, and, if so, which of the following different effects on the opponent receiving serve could be considered?

A First serve: Take a little **speed off the hit** to upset timing.

B First serve forehand side: Try to **play it wide** to take the opponent out of court.

C Second serve: Try to **aim it to swerve** into the player's body to upset his technique.

D Second serve: Try to keep the ball **bouncing low** to make the opponent bend.

Q11 Adapting your normal flat serve to incorporate slice can be a tricky problem to overcome. What technical points need to be observed to adapt your normal serve and make it a successful slice serve?

A The ball toss needs to be **placed further to the left** than on a normal serve.

B The ball toss needs to be **slightly further back.**

C The racket face needs to be **flat on contact.**

D You should try to **cut the right-hand edge** of the ball.

Q12 On most flat shots the racket face points toward the target area on the forward swing (in the hitting zone). However, when you are trying to hit the ball with spin you are intentionally hitting it slightly on the side, which means your racket face is not aiming toward the hitting zone. What do you need to do to hit the ball in court (right-handed servers)?

A Hit the ball **harder.**

B Aim slightly **higher** over the net.

C Aim further to the **right.**

D Change to a **closed stance.**

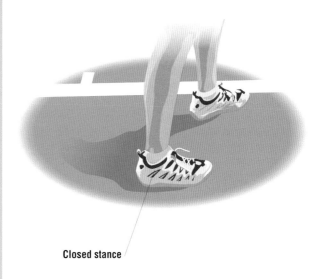

Closed stance

29

player   *opponent*

Answer: A C E

A9

The tactical advantages gained by a player who can spin the ball with slice on the serve are many and varied, and will in most situations give the player returning serve a variety of problems to overcome. The flight of the ball in the air will swing more, and after the bounce the ball will swing from the server's right to left (returner's left to right). This should cause the returner difficulty in judging the movement of the ball, which could result in him having difficulty in setting up an efficient technique. The ball will be moving into his body on the backhand side and away from his body on the forehand side. A steady first-serve hit with a little slice

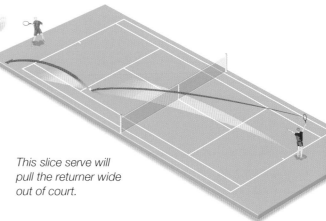

This slice serve will pull the returner wide out of court.

will cause the ball to bounce lower than usual, upsetting the opponent's judgment. Slice on the second serve can enable a player to hit a steady safe serve, which can, however, force the opponent into a defensive situation.

Answer: A B C D

A10

Hitting a first serve with slice and taking off a little speed (A) is a great tactic, since most returners are not expecting a change of spin and speed on your first serve. Hitting a first serve with slice wide into the forehand court (B) is a great tactic for pulling your opponent outside his sidelines, which can then leave a large opening for your next shot. Second serve into the body (C). When you aim at the backhand side of your opponent you will be swinging the ball into the body, which can restrict his ability to generate pace and cramp his swing. Second serve, slice low (D). If you can keep your opponent hitting returns from below net height you have put him on the defensive.

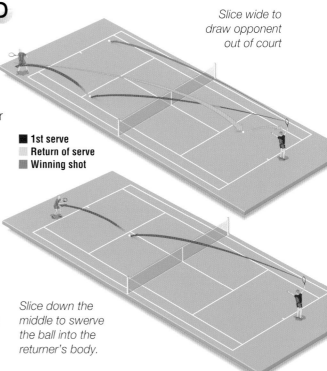

Slice wide to draw opponent out of court

■ 1st serve
▨ Return of serve
■ Winning shot

Slice down the middle to swerve the ball into the returner's body.

A11

Answer: D

If you can visualize the ball when you hit it as being a clock face, it may help you to have a better picture of the differences between a flat and a slice serve. On contact, on a flat serve the racket face will hit all the numbers simultaneously. On a slice-serve contact the racket will appear to chop off numbers 1–5 leaving 12–6 intact. This will send the ball spinning through the air, which then creates the swing in flight. You need to place the ball toss further to the right (and slightly further forward) than normal to enable you to hit the side of the ball more easily and create the slice effect.

Flat serve

Slice serve

A12

Answer: B C

As most players progress they need variations in their game to create tactical advantages. This requires them to adapt their basic techniques to incorporate new shots into their tactical plan. The problems facing a player trying to add a slice serve to their tactical play are mainly a loss of control or ability to direct the ball accurately to a target area. When players first use slice they find that they spin the ball, but generally it goes into the bottom of the net and approximately 20 feet (6m) to the left. (This is because they have changed the angle of the racket face on contact from their normal angle.) No matter how hard they try, it is almost impossible to get it over the net. In the beginning you need to aim approximately 20 feet (6m) toward the right of where you want the ball to go and about 6–12 feet (1.8–3.6m) above net height. You should find that now your slice will go into court.

Serve direction

Aim to the right of where you want the ball to go.

2.4 Using **spin** for effect—**topspin**

If you are a competent club player with an aggressive first serve, it is frustrating if you have a weak second serve that your opponents attack easily. If this is you, then you definitely need a topspin second serve.

Ball breaks to one side with increased racket speed

■ Normal serve
■ Topspin serve

Q13 Can you use topspin as a tactical advantage on both your first and second serves? Which of the following tactical effects should be considered?

A First serve: Use a slightly **slower topspin** serve to upset rhythm.

B First serve: Try to make the **ball shoot through lower.**

C Second serve: Try to develop **less spin** and reduce the bounce.

D Second serve: With increased racket-head speed you can **"break"** (kick) the ball to one side.

Q14 When you are using topspin effectively as a tactical weapon on the serve, the flight of the ball in the air and the spin of the ball after the bounce should challenge and upset your opponent's timing, positions, and rhythm. Which of the following answers are true?

Direction of ball

Velocity

Topspin

A The ball will **rotate in the air** and dip downward quickly.

B After the bounce the ball will **bounce lower** than normal.

C Topspin enables you to hit the ball **higher and harder** but still keep it in play.

Q15

The techniques of the topspin serve are based on the competent basic serve. It does require a number of changes in a player's basic technique. Which of the following points will benefit a topspin serve?

D The player should try to "brush up" the back of the ball with the racket face.

A The ball toss needs to be **further back** than normal.

B The ball toss needs to be **behind the player's head.**

C The player's **back should be arched.**

E The player should **accelerate the racket head** (through impact) more than normal.

F Aim **higher** over the net and to the right of your target area.

Q16

Developing a topspin serve from scratch is an interesting challenge for most players. Which of the following teaching points would help you to develop the skill?

E Practice for **long periods** to develop consistency.

A Practice in your **friendly doubles match.**

B Count **how many serves** you hit into court.

C Try to **exaggerate and increase** the amount of spin (rotation) on the ball.

D If you can play a **topspin forehand** successfully, transfer this knowledge to the serve.

A13

Answer: A D

When you first start introducing the topspin serve into your tactical play, it may not necessarily give you a big advantage until you have refined

A "kick serve" bounces and kicks to the right.

your technique, However, it is always important first to know what to do as a tactic and then try to master the technique. On your first serve, when your opponent is expecting a fast flat serve, it is a good moment to outwit him with a change of pace and spin to upset his rhythm. Also, why not try to direct your serve at a possible weakness (high-ball bounces to a single-handed backhand or a weak forehand)? On your second serve try to spin the ball faster to develop a higher bounce and put your opponent in the defensive position (outside his baseline).

If you develop this further it can lead into a "kick serve," whereby the ball also breaks to the right after the bounce.

A14

Answer: A C

The modern game of tennis requires players to hit the ball aggressively and yet make few mistakes. Topspin used effectively allows players to hit the ball very hard but keeps the ball safely in court. How can this topspin have such a beneficial effect? When a player hits the ball with topspin the ball rotates forward (spins) in the air. These rotations force the ball downward in flight more quickly than

a normal flat shot. When the ball hits the ground the rotations have the effect of making it bounce higher off the ground than is usually the case. This means that, once you have perfected the topspin serve, you will be able to hit the ball higher over the net and/or harder than normal, but still keep it in the service box.

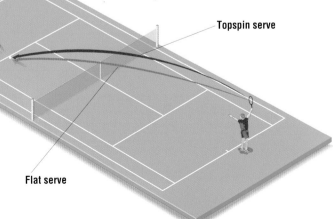

Topspin serve

Flat serve

Answer: A B C D E F

All the answers need to be applied to achieve tactical competence on the topspin serve. Comparing the racket-throwing action on the flat serve to a topspin serve is possible if you visualize the difference by imagining the ball as a clock face. On the flat serve you will hit all the numbers on the clock face. On the topspin serve your racket face will come from below the numbers 6–9, brush upward across the clock face, and leave between 12 and 3. This action will rotate the ball forward and bring topspin into play. It will require a faster action than usual to achieve an effective brushing action.

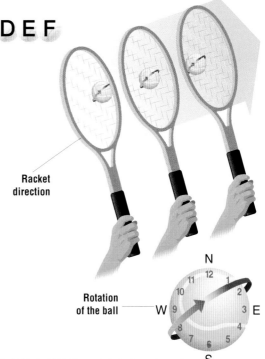

Racket direction

Rotation of the ball

Answer: C D

When you are trying to learn a new technique, especially a variation of an existing one, you will most likely make many mistakes. The old adage "You learn by your mistakes" is true. Don't be frightened of errors, because you can learn from each one. The real hurdle to improvement is when players feel embarrassed, threatened, or inadequate through making mistakes. What you need is a plan of action that will retain your self-confidence through the frustrations and successes of learning a new skill. So:

Practice quietly on your own away from the eyes of possible critical watchers.
Try to learn from your mistakes; take your time and don't count how many misses you make.
Keep working on spin rotation—listen to the different noise of topspin.
If you can play topspin forehand, relate the technique to your serve.

Ball rotation in a topspin forehand

Ball rotation in a topspin serve

2.5 Serve-and-volley

Players who are competent at match play will find this particular tactic very helpful, especially when they are playing doubles. If you can master this tactic you will find you have added an extra dimension to your game and created new challenges for your opponents.

Q17 Deciding when to use serve-and-volley as a tactic is often a difficult decision to make for an intermediate player. Which of the following factors should you consider to make your tactic more effective?

A On your **first serve.**

B On your **second serve.**

C On an **"important"** point.

D Aiming at your opponent's **weaker side.**

Q18 When you have decided to serve-and-volley, you need to make some adjustments to your normal basic serving technique, because you are going to be moving swiftly to the net once you have hit the serve. What techniques should you adjust to make it a successful tactic?

A **Jump** in the air.

B Place the ball **further forward** than normal.

C Make sure that you have **forward momentum.**

D Start **running forward** during the serve.

Q19 The serve-and-volley technique requires very quick movement away from the serving position to achieve a sound volleying position at the front of the court. What points should we consider to develop speed and stability?

A The follow-through of the feet should be **into the court.**

B Sprint to in front of the **service line.**

C Sprint to the **net position.**

D Sprint and check into a **ready position** as your opponent strikes the ball.

Q20 Many players experience difficulty with the first volley when using this tactic. Because they are trying to make an attacking position they can end up making too many mistakes. What do you need to consider with your volleying to make this tactic a success?

A Play the ball very **close to your body.**

B Try to play the ball with a **balanced hitting position.**

C If your volley is above waist height, **try to hit a winner.**

D If your volley is low, play **carefully for position.**

E Keep running **forward** as you play the volley.

Overall movement for serve and volley.

If your volley is low play carefully for position.

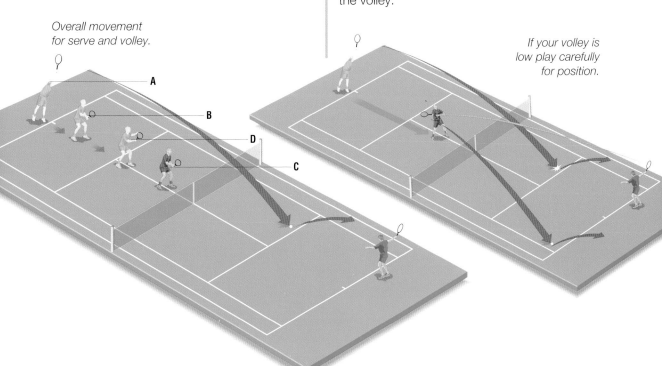

Answer: A D

The serve-and-volley tactic can be very effective for intermediate players with a reasonably sound attacking serve. This tactic is probably easier for most players to use in doubles because they have a smaller target area to cover. Because their partner is covering half the court, this tactic should be developed on all court surfaces to achieve a position where both players are in a strong position together at the net.

When you first start using this tactic it is advisable to use it on your stronger first serve only, and try to direct your serve to your opponent's weaker side. It may be necessary to take a little speed off your first serve to ensure that it goes into play regularly on to a weakness. In the early stages don't serve-and-volley all the time; keep your opponents guessing, which can lead to errors in their returns.

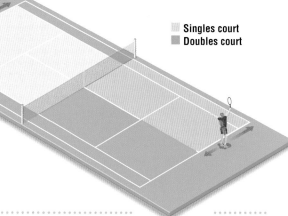

■ Singles court
■ Doubles court

Answer: B C

The technical adjustments you need to make to your service action when you incorporate it into your serve-and-volley tactic are quite small but they are extremely important.

When you serve normally, your body weight should transfer toward the target area. In this situation you have decided you are following the ball to the net, so your forward momentum is the starting point for your first explosive sprint step toward the net. You will need to place your ball toss further in front than normal to develop a fluid throwing action of your racket, which then continues your body momentum forward. You also need to make sure you strike the ball at maximum height using your legs to push up and elevate your body (ground reaction force) into its optimum contact position.

Fluid throwing action of the racket with B and C.

Answer: A D

When you watch the forward movement to the net by an accomplished serve-and-volleyer, it looks so fluid and coordinated. However, the action can be broken down into five segments:

1. Service action

2. Sprint—approximately to service line

3. Check into a ready position

4. Play a first volley

5. Sprint to net position and check into ready position for second volley.

The serve and the sprint appear straightforward, but when do you check into the ready position? Take a stable, balanced ready position just before your opponent makes contact with her return. On a slow serve or if you are a fast sprinter you could play the first volley inside the service box; if you play a fast serve or are quite slow you will probably play your first volley outside the box. You then repeat the sprint, taking position for your second volley at the net.

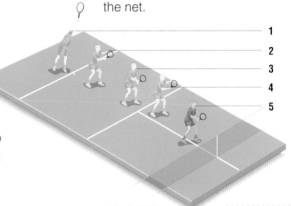

Answer: B D

One of the first difficulties you may experience with this technique is caused by your sprint forward, which significantly decreases the distance between your opponent and yourself and also decreases the time you have to set up your first shot, the first volley. The following technique pointers need to be taken into account if you want this tactic to be a success.

Your ready position for a first volley needs to be a balanced position ready to play a low volley. You need to play the ball well in front of your body, which can lead into your forward momentum to set up a good position for your second volley. Against a serve-and-volley tactic, most returners will try to aim the ball low over the net toward the feet of the incoming volleyer. Be prepared for this and aim your low volley carefully for a deep position in your opponent's court.

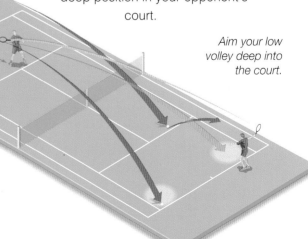

Aim your low volley deep into the court.

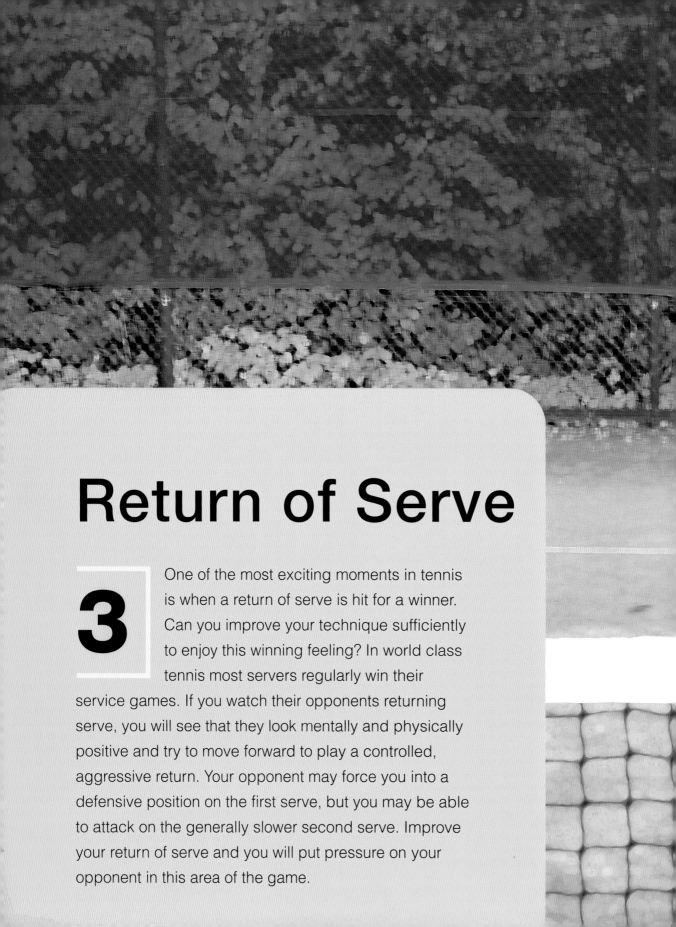

Return of Serve

3

One of the most exciting moments in tennis is when a return of serve is hit for a winner. Can you improve your technique sufficiently to enjoy this winning feeling? In world class tennis most servers regularly win their service games. If you watch their opponents returning serve, you will see that they look mentally and physically positive and try to move forward to play a controlled, aggressive return. Your opponent may force you into a defensive position on the first serve, but you may be able to attack on the generally slower second serve. Improve your return of serve and you will put pressure on your opponent in this area of the game.

3.1

Return of first serve in singles—**basic positioning**

Developing an efficient return of first serve is vital if you are to improve your tennis game. The first serve is a fast and powerful shot, so you must position yourself strategically if you are to make a good return.

Q1 When playing a singles match, where is the most sensible position to stand to receive serve?

A Near the **sideline**.

B Near the **center line**.

C **Halfway** between A and B.

D About 6½ feet (2m) **behind** the baseline.

E Diagonally **opposite** your opponent.

F Near the **baseline**.

Q2 This is a difficult shot to play, with the server attacking you with speed and direction. What are the percentage options to keep you in the point and perhaps develop your own attack?

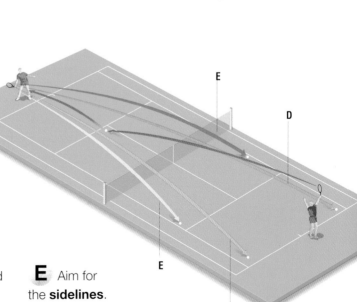

A Try to hit a **winner**.

B Return the ball **deep**.

C Hit **harder** than the server.

D Aim toward the **corners**.

E Aim for the **sidelines**.

Q3 Keeping your balance when you play your shot is an important factor in developing power and accuracy. Which of the following will help to develop this aspect of your game?

A Do a **split step** prior to moving.

B Play the ball **sideways** on.

C Always go **forward** to meet the ball.

Q4 Many players find returning a fast serve difficult. The speed of the ball can upset their speed, rhythm, and control. Which of the following technical adjustments would make your return more consistent and accurate?

A Taking a **full backswing**.

B Watching the **opponent's positioning**.

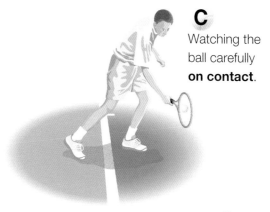

C Watching the ball carefully **on contact**.

D Playing the ball **well in front** of your body with your wrist firm.

opponent

 player

Answer: E F

Under the rules of tennis, the receiver may stand wherever he wishes on his side of the court. The position taken by most players is one diagonally opposite the server. If you were to imagine a piece of string tied to server and receiver, this string should bisect the service court (see right) and enable equal coverage of forehand and backhand sides. However, you then have to take into account servers' favorite target areas and returners' weaker return areas. These may cause you to adjust your basic position slightly.

When returning serve, stand diagonally opposite the server.

Answers: B D

When the server is hitting the first serve it is most likely that the returner is going to be in a defensive situation when playing his return. This is where percentage play should come into effect. The percentage odds are against the returner, so he should settle for putting the ball into play and hopefully putting his opponent under pressure. The two safest options are:

1. To return the ball deep to keep your opponent behind his baseline.

2. To aim toward the corners to force your opponent away from his central ready position.

■ **Try to return the ball in this area to force server onto defensive**

■ **Safest place for returner to aim toward**

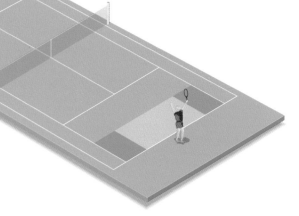

Answer: A C

The split step in tennis is used as a method of helping players to use "ground reaction force" by pushing against the ground for maximum thrust and a quick start, enabling them to move swiftly, both forward/backward and side to side. As the opponent is about to make contact with his serve, the returner should jump slightly off the ground. As the server contacts the ball, the returner should have landed on both feet and be poised ready to move— forward to the ball and diagonally sideways as necessary.

Do a split step prior to moving. Pushing against the ground will give you a quick start as you return serve.

Answer: C D

Remember the five golden tactics of tennis:

1. Hit the ball
2. Over the net
3. Into the court
4. Away from your opponent
5. With speed

As you can see, the first four are all about controlling the ball through effective technique. You need to play the ball well in front of the body with a firm control of your wrist on contact with the ball (D). If your wrist is too loose on contact, points 2, 3, and 4 above will probably fail. Remember, you need to try to watch the ball all the way to your racket to ensure that you have adjusted your swing (C). As your opponent is hitting a first serve with speed, you will probably not require Tactic 5 unless you want to hit the ball exceptionally hard.

When waiting to return serve, be alert and watch the direction of the ball very carefully.

45

3.2

Returning the first serve—**server staying back**

This is the time when the opponent is totally in control of her situation, with the ball in her hand, knowing she can attack the serve because she has a second chance if she fails with her first. You need a cool head to overcome her tactical advantage.

Q5

When you are playing against a strong first serve it is difficult to play your normal baseline game because of the speed of that serve. So where should you position yourself for maximum tactical effect?

A **On** the baseline.

B **Just outside** the baseline—3.3 feet (1m).

C **Outside** the baseline—6.6 feet (2m).

D **Outside** the baseline —9.8 feet (3m).

Q6

When returning a fast first serve, the returner is often under great pressure and feels tactically at a loss, not knowing where to hit the ball. Which of the following tactics could help to improve this area of your play?

A Hit straight **down** the line.

B Hit short **across** court.

C Hit down the **middle.**

D Hit high and **deep across court.**

E Hit high and **deep down the middle.**

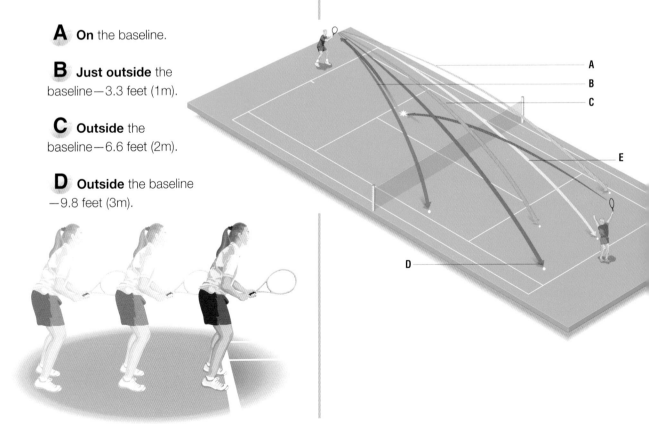

When trying to return a first serve, many players experience difficulty in anticipating where the ball is directed and in judging the speed accurately. Which of the following might speed up your reactions?

 Because the player returning the first serve has little time, there needs to be some adjustment in the basic technique. Which of the following adjustments may be helpful for the improving player?

A More alert ready position.

B Playing the ball more in **front of the body.**

C Keeping the body weight **moving forward** into the shot.

A Anticipate a **pattern** in direction.

B Compare the pattern of **direction** in the forehand court to the backhand court.

C Look for clues in the **ball toss**.

D Check to see if the ball is **spinning** in flight.

D Shortening the backswing.

E Keeping the wrist **firm but flexible.**

F **Swinging more slowly** than normal.

player *opponent*

The returner takes a ready position 6½ feet (2m) behind the baseline but moves forward to play the return on the baseline.

Answer: B C

A5

Returning serve against a strong first serve requires some tactical positioning of your ready position. As a general principle take up your normal ready position to return, and then if necessary on subsequent returns adjust your position until you feel you have more time. When you feel comfortable on your returns, try gradually to regain your original position.

Answer: D E

A6

In this situation most returners are under pressure and are being put into a defensive situation by the speed of the opponent's serve. Don't be too ambitious, but try to return the ball deep into the opponent's court. Try to control the return by taking some speed off the ball, and try to hit higher over the net than normal. If you do this you may put your opponent on the defensive and improve your chance of winning the point.

The returner is playing a high and deep return up the middle of the court to force the server onto the defensive.

Answer: A B C

A7

Returning a fast first serve requires excellent anticipation and ball-judgment skills. Because of the speed you probably have only 1½ seconds to judge, react, move, and hit either a forehand or backhand return of serve. If you can extend this time by anticipating which side the server may be aiming toward before they hit the ball, you may gain a precious half-second. Sometimes the positioning of the ball toss can give away the direction of the serve.

Try to anticipate the server's intention by looking at the positioning of the ball.

Answer: A B C D

The receiver has less time than normal to construct an efficient forehand or backhand when returning a fast first serve. Some small adjustments to the basic technique will be needed to gain time to play an efficient return.

Adopt a more positive and aggressive ready position in order to move forward to play the ball. You need to contact with the ball well in front of the body, which will enable your momentum to go forward into the shot.

Since the ball is traveling much faster than normal, you don't require a large backswing to gain speed, so shorten your backswing as much as necessary to hit the ball in front of your body.

The player should move forward to play the return, but retaining balance, which will increase the accuracy of shot.

Return of Serve

3.3
Returning the second serve — **server back**

The server should be in the attacking position on the first serve, while the attacking options shift to the returner on the second serve. The second serve can be attacked with pace and variety by the player returning it, if some of the tactical and technical fundamentals are followed.

Q9 This should be your **opportunity to attack the second serve. Your opponent needs to put the ball into play and will probably take a lot of speed off his shot. If you can take advantage of this opportunity, you have an excellent chance of winning the point. What should you consider as part of your tactics?**

A Moving your returning **position further up the court than normal.**

B Positioning yourself **on the baseline.**

C Developing **forward momentum** during the shot.

Q10 Many players find difficulty in successfully attacking the second serve. It is often a short ball with little speed, and yet so often the returner makes a mistake by hitting it into the net or out of the court. What are the tactical options available in this situation?

A Hit **down the line** and follow to the net.

B Hit **crosscourt** and follow to the net.

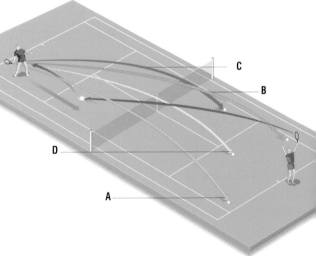

C Hit **crosscourt** short angle.

D Hit **down the middle** and follow to the net.

Q11 Most club players around team standard will put a little spin on their second serve to make it more difficult for the opposition. The two main spins used are slice and topspin, which cause the ball to take significantly different flight paths and spin off the ground. How can you pick up any clues from the server's technique?

A Watch the **ball toss** compared with first serve.

B Shape of the **server's backswing and throwing action.**

C The **arch and bend** of the server's back.

D The **flight or swing** of the ball.

Topspin   Normal   Slice

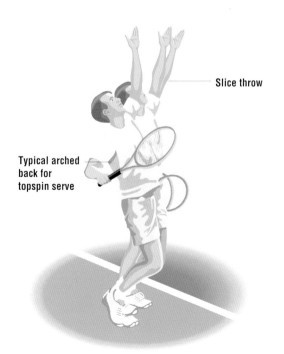

Slice throw

Typical arched back for topspin serve

Q12 Now is the moment for the player returning the serve to take control of the point if the second serve is easy to attack. This is the time to be positive and play with controlled aggression added to your strengths. The percentages are in your favor, but what techniques do you mainly need to consider?

A Use **more topspin.**

B Aim **closer** to the net.

C **Prepare** early.

D Take a **full backswing.**

E **Move forward** early.

F Watch the ball very closely on contact.

51

Answer: A C

Generally, at the beginner/improver level, the second serve is played quite slowly by the server to ensure that it goes in the service box. This gives the opponent the opportunity to attack what is a short-length ball. As a general principle, stand on or just inside the baseline to be ready for the shorter length ball. When you move forward to the second serve, make sure you continue this balanced momentum into the shot so you can hit the returns into a variety of positions on court.

The player moves forward to attack the second serve.

Answer: A C

Probably the most difficult ball for the server to defend against is the return of serve down the line with the returner following the shot to the net in order to volley. This return gives the server less time to cover his court and gives him limited angles for his attempts at passing shots. The next best option for the returner on a wide second serve is to play a short crosscourt angle aiming toward the corner of the service box. This will pull the server wide out of court to return the ball, leaving a large area of court open for the returner's next shot.

Top: A crosscourt return of serve.
Bottom: Down the line return of serve.

Answer: A B

Most team players will be proficient at putting at least one type of spin on their serves. The better team players will generally be able to hit their serves with either topspin or slice. This is where it is very difficult to anticipate and read what spin is going to be used unless you watch your opponent's service technique very carefully. Watch the direction of the ball toss as a guide to a possible spin, and try to pick up the shape of the backswing and throwing action. You will probably see a pattern emerging that can give you advance warning.

Slice serve

Topspin serve—note the arched back at the start

Answer: A C D

What are your challenges in this situation? You are hitting probably more aggressively than usual and hitting from inside your court (a shorter distance than normal). It is so easy to overhit the ball and make an unforced error. Try to prepare earlier, moving forward to the ball to retain your balance and momentum. You now need to put topspin on the ball to ensure that you:
1. Hit hard and keep it in play.
2. Play a crosscourt short-angle shot using more topspin and taking a little of the speed off your shot.

Movement of ball with topspin

Movement of hand/racket

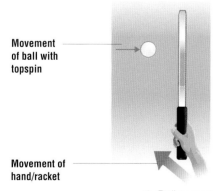

1. Ball comes toward racket.

2. Ball makes contact with racket.

3. Racket brushes up behind ball.

4. Ball leaves racket with topspin.

3.4

Against
a serve volleyer

Most players who use the tactics of serve-and-volley will probably have a fast first serve. You need to try to return every serve over the net and force them to play a volley. If you can do this regularly you will find it easier to break their serve.

A Aim straight **at the volleyer**.

B Aim **at the feet** of the volleyer.

C Aim approximately **6½ feet (2m)** from the sidelines.

Q13 When you are returning **against** a serve-and-volley player, **which of the following tactics are considered the best tactics?**

Q14 What groundstroke, technical changes should you, as returner, employ in order to be most effective in dipping the ball at the feet of the serve volleyer, or passing him?

C Take a **shorter** backswing.

A Take a **longer** backswing.

B Take a **normal** backswing.

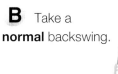

D Keep your **balance** and move to the ball.

Q15

Many players disagree over the best tactics to use against the serve volleyer. Which is better—topspin or slice? And which of the following are the best tactics?

A Hit your **normal shot**.

B Try to use **more topspin**.

C Try to **use slice** and chip the ball.

D Hit **without spin**.

■ Service
░ Topspin return
■ Normal shot
■ Slice

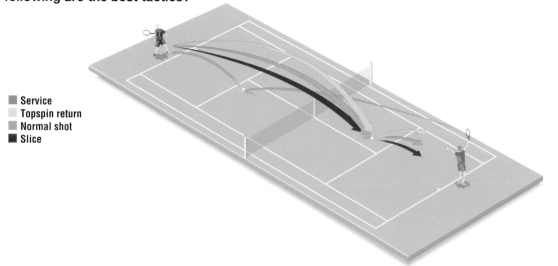

Q16

Many players returning serve think only of their first shot and can be very surprised when their opponent makes his "good" return with a solid volley. Which of the following second shots could be considered a sound option in doubles?

C Trying to hit **between opponents**.

D Follow your **dipping return** to the net.

Ball hit between the two opponents

A Hitting a **deep return**.

B Expecting opponent's volley **on your weaker side**.

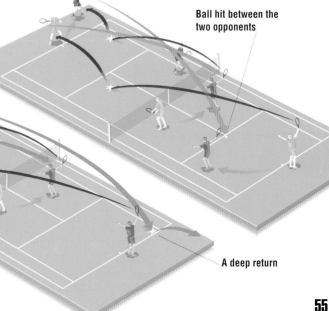

A deep return

■ *player*　■ *opponent*

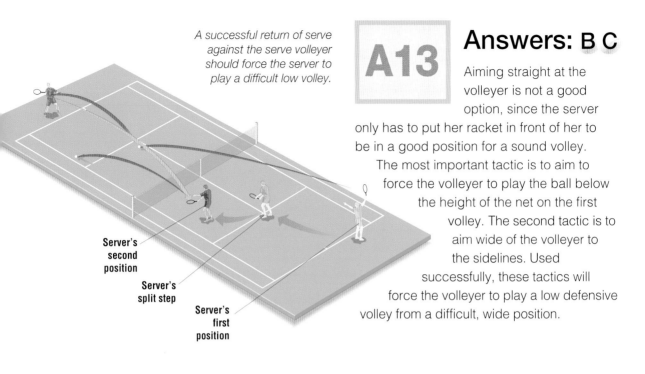

A successful return of serve against the serve volleyer should force the server to play a difficult low volley.

Server's
second
position

Server's
split step

Server's
first
position

Answers: B C

A13

Aiming straight at the volleyer is not a good option, since the server only has to put her racket in front of her to be in a good position for a sound volley. The most important tactic is to aim to force the volleyer to play the ball below the height of the net on the first volley. The second tactic is to aim wide of the volleyer to the sidelines. Used successfully, these tactics will force the volleyer to play a low defensive volley from a difficult, wide position.

The most important factor in combating a serve-and-volleyer is to retain your balance and forward momentum throughout your shot.

Answers: C D

A14

Playing against a serve-and-volley player you need the techniques and skills to "dip" the ball over the net and down at the volleyer's feet. Balance is probably the most important factor in controlling the height and direction of the return. When returning, try to keep your head still and your body momentum going forward (and your wrist firm) when you play the shot. You will not need a full backswing to achieve the necessary power. Remember, you are hitting the ball only 75 percent of your normal distance, and accuracy is more important than power in this situation.

A15

Answers: B C

When playing against a serve volleyer the return of serve needs to be aimed to land near the service line. The most difficult ball for the returner to play is one that lands near her feet and below net height, and has very little speed. The topspin return is the more aggressive return, since it is hit faster through the air with forward spin, dipping sharply down in its flight. The slice return is the more gentle and subtle return, traveling more slowly through the air with backspin, gently dipping down in its flight. This situation is best played with either heavy topspin or a little slice. It depends on which method you feel more comfortable and secure with.

Use your favorite spin (either topspin or slice) to force the server to play a difficult low volley.

Topspin return

Normal return

Server

Ball with topspin

Ball with slice (backspin)

A16

Answers: B C

Somebody once described tennis as "a game of chess on the move." Others have described it as a battle with attack, defense, and counterattack. In all instances, players need to be thinking ahead and anticipating their opponents' moves and responses. When returning in doubles against a serve volleyer the returner knows the volleyer will generally play the ball back as a deep crosscourt shot, and, if possible, to his weaker side. This is where he should have planned his second shot as early as possible, with the percentage shot aimed between his opponents.

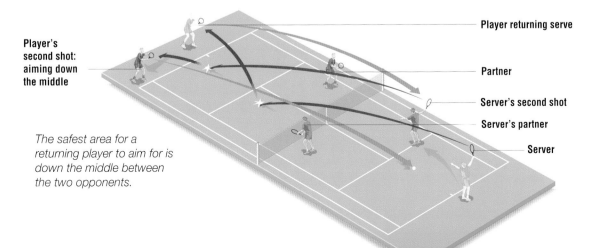

Player's second shot: aiming down the middle

The safest area for a returning player to aim for is down the middle between the two opponents.

Player returning serve

Partner

Server's second shot

Server's partner

Server

Both Players Back

4 This area of play is the follow-up to the serve and return, with the ball in play and both players hitting ground strokes from around the baseline area. Now players are probing for weakness in their opponent's game, looking for a chance to attack and win the point. You need to show controlled aggression and reduce your errors to a minimum until you get the opportunity to attack. You must also be consistent on both forehand and backhand sides if you want to dominate the point. Top players are successful in this area because they plan their strategy, playing to their own strengths and exposing their opponent's weaknesses.

4.1 Ground stroke techniques—the **forehand**

For most players, the forehand is their favorite shot. You should aim to develop a forehand that is safe and strong in defensive positions but also aggressive and consistent from attacking positions.

Q1

It is quite difficult for many novice tennis players to decide what is the best method to grip the racket. Watching top players play can be quite confusing, with the variety of grips used. Which of the following is most suitable?

A **Continental** grip.

B **Eastern** grip.

C **Semiwestern** grip.

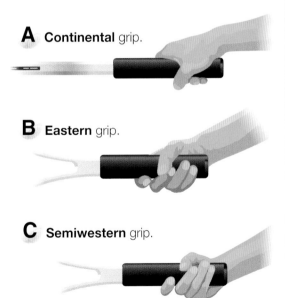

D **Western** grip.

Q2

When you are waiting for your opponent to hit his shot, you need to be in an "alert-ready position" in order to move quickly in any direction to hit your next shot. How should you stand to be quick off the mark?

A On the **balls** of your feet.

B Feet approximately **shoulder-width** apart.

C Feet **close** together.

D **One foot behind** the other.

It is generally assumed that the racket backswing is prepared in a rhythmical and continuous manner. Which is probably the best shape of backswing to adopt in order to develop a sound and flexible technique? From the ready position, how should you take the racket back?

A Low—high—low.

B Low—level—level.

C High—low—high.

 Control and accuracy generally come from a sound forward swing, especially in the important area of the "hitting zone," which is the area of 2 feet (0.6m) before contact and 2 feet (0.6m) after contact. Where is generally accepted to be the best stance on the forehand drive to set up a sound contact position?

A Feet **sideways** on.

B Feet **open** stance.

C Feet **semi-open** stance.

Answer: B C

These two grips are most suitable for most players to use effectively in a wide range of situations. It is a personal choice as to which grip to use, but it will depend on your style of play and your personal technique. The continental grip will not be suitable for topspin play and the full western grip will be suitable only for heavy topspin play. Most top players who are successful on a variety of different court surfaces will tend to use the semiwestern forehand grip. This grip leads to hitting successfully with topspin

The two most effective grips are the eastern and the semiwestern.

or a flat shot, either of which is one of the main weapons of attacking play.

Eastern grip

Semiwestern grip

Your alert-ready position should enable you to move quickly in any direction.

Answer: A B

From the moment your opponent hits his shot, you have approximately one second to judge the ball, prepare your racket, decide your tactic, and hit your next shot. As you can see, there is a lot to consider in a very short space of time. This is when the alert-ready position will give you that little extra edge you need. The majority of shots will not come direct to you, so you must be prepared to push off the ground quickly in any direction. You also need your racket across the front of your body, supported with the spare hand, so you are ready to play either forehand or backhand shots.

A3

Answer: C

This method of take-back to a high position (approximately shoulder height), followed by letting the racket at its fullest extension fall to a low position, leads to a natural looped swing. This then moves into a smooth climbing or lifted shot, which is the basic form for the topspin or lifted forehand. However, by lessening the fall of the racket on the backswing, this take-back can easily be adapted to play a slice shot, because it will create a slightly downward and forward swing, which is a sound base for such a shot.

A smooth, flowing backswing is the key to a successful forehand stroke.

A semi-open stance allows you to hit down the line or crosscourt with only a slight adjustment in contact point.

A4

Answer: C

Generally, a semi-open stance is considered to be the most effective and versatile position for the forehand drive. This stance will allow you to hit the shot accurately and forcefully, whether it is down the line or crosscourt, with only a slight change in your contact point. To achieve the change of direction the semi-open stance will also assist the transfer of your bodyweight (momentum) into the shot. As a general principle, your contact point should always be in front of your body, approximately level with, or forward of, your front hip.

4.2

The **two-handed backhand**

Players often prefer the two-handed backhand because of the strength the second hand brings. The downside of this method is loss of reach, as well as its greater physical demand. Try both methods and decide which one is for you.

Q5

The two-handed backhand can be a very powerful shot if you have a firm but flexible grip. What are your best options for your grips on both hands?

A Two forehand grips **touching**.

B Two forehand grips **interlocking**.

C Two eastern forehand grips **apart**.

D One **continental** forehand grip and one **eastern** forehand grip.

Q6

It is generally assumed with the two-handed backhand that the momentum in the hitting zone should be toward the target, and yet many top-class players tend to jump and rotate during the shot. Which of the following points should you consider during your forward swing?

A Keeping **both feet** on the ground.

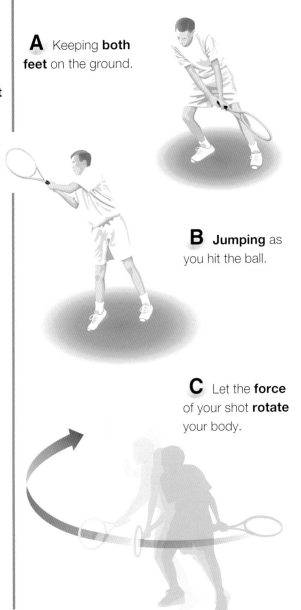

B **Jumping** as you hit the ball.

C Let the **force** of your shot **rotate** your body.

Q7 Watching top players prepare for a two-handed backhand, you see many varying setups for the shot. Which of the following backswings appear most appropriate for control and power?

Q8 Two-handed players will have a problem with balls that are bouncing low, especially when they have to stretch for a wide one. What techniques should they use in order to overcome this problem?

A Straight take-back.

A Play a **single-handed** recovery shot.

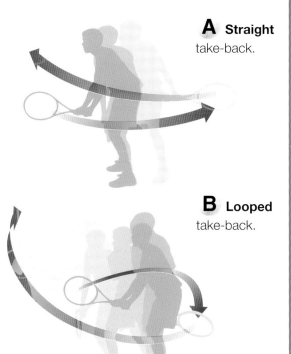

B Looped take-back.

B Bend lower than normal.

C **Short** looped take-back.

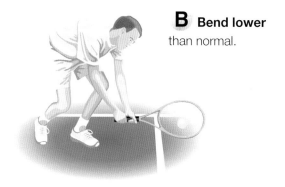

C Hit the ball at its **highest point**.

D Long take-back.

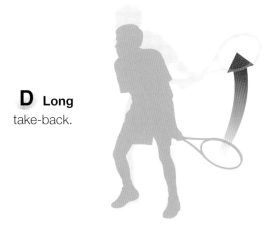

D Always use **two hands**.

Two eastern forehand grips touching

One continental forehand grip and one eastern forehand grip

Answer: A D

A5

The novice player will generally start with two eastern forehand grips, because these will feel most comfortable. The problem is that in the long term it is very difficult to develop topspin on the shot with this grip. By adjusting the hand on the bottom to a continental forehand grip, it is now possible to add more topspin to the shot. This can then lead to hitting the ball with more power and still keeping it in play. So, if you are unsure, start with Grip A and, when you have developed some basic control, try to move on to Grip D—the preferred grip.

Answer: A C

A6

Novice players who are trying to develop control and consistency will generally not be hitting the ball very hard. They will need a stable base and will mainly be using Method A. As players progress they will be looking to hit the ball with more power and topspin. This requires the racket head to be accelerating through the hitting zone with the left hand more dominant. As the left arm follows through across the body, this will create a rotational force, leaning to the back leg, and following around, with the body rotating—the whole move creating an impression of a jump during the shot.

A balanced position allows you to rotate your body as you take the shot.

■ player   ■ opponent

Answer: B D

Tennis techniques can often be described as a trade-off between control and power. If you want to hit the ball hard you ideally need a long backswing to develop racket-head speed. You also need to develop a smooth coordinated flow between backswing and forward swing **(1)** to gain maximum force with minimum effort. However, if you wish to hit the ball accurately but softly you can manage with a short backswing and a straight take-back **(2)**. So what's best? With a

long backswing and smooth coordinated flow you can, by slowing down the swing, still hit the ball slowly and carefully; but with a short backswing you will never generate enough racket-head speed to hit the ball hard.

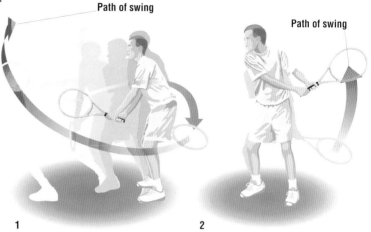

Path of swing

Path of swing

1   2

Answer: A

Most two-handed players would love to answer this question with Answers B and C. This would be their ideal situation if they were fast enough to reach the ball and play it with their most efficient technique. However, in the real world, we have to improvise. By releasing the left hand from the racket, you will automatically increase your reach, whether it is low or wide. This will enable you to play a sliced single-handed backhand as a "rescue"

shot. This ball is probably very low and/or wide. It makes the technique quite difficult, especially for a two-handed player who is now not using his dominant hand. Tactically, you should try to keep the ball in play, probably hitting a lob to keep your opponent at the back of the court, which will give you time to recover to a good court position.

You can reach a difficult ball by releasing one of your hands to play a sliced single-handed backhand as a "rescue shot."

4.3 The **one-handed backhand**

Some players feel uncomfortable with both hands on the racket, or simply prefer this method, which allows a range of variations. However, with only one hand holding the racket you will need to set up your shot very efficiently to achieve optimum power and control.

Q9 Compared with the forehand, many novice players feel awkward and weak on the single-handed backhand. This can lead to mishitting the ball and loss of direction and control. Which grip is the best for overcoming some of these problems?

A The **eastern forehand** grip—shaking-hands grip.

B The **backhand** grip— knuckle behind grip.

C The **continental** grip (halfway between A and B).

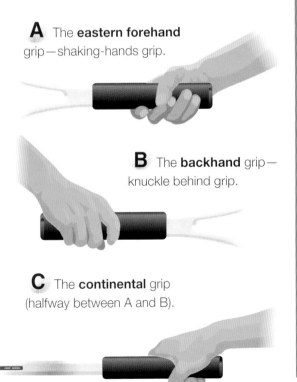

Q10 It is generally assumed that the best place to contact the ball is in front of you. This can be somewhat vague advice. Where exactly should the ball be contacted for maximum control and power? Which three of the following six answers are most appropriate?

A At **knee height**.

B At **waist height**.

C **Opposite** the leading leg.

D In **front** of the leading leg.

E A comfortable **arm's length** from the body.

F With a **straight arm**.

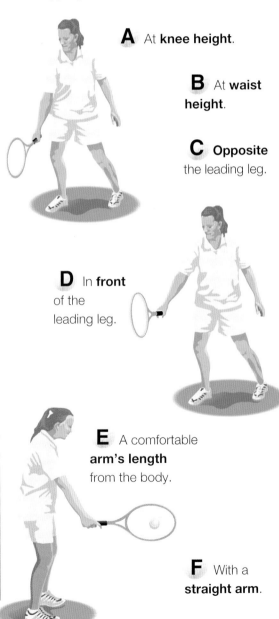

Q11 Using the left hand on the single-handed backhand is usually recommended to aid control of the racket head during take-back. At what stage should the left hand be taken away and stop supporting the racket?

A As the **body turns**.

B At the top of the **backswing**.

C On the **loop** downward.

D At the **beginning** of the forward swing.

Q12 You will probably hear conflicting advice on whether you should use your wrist in your shots. How much wrist should be used on the basic single-handed backhand?

A **None** at all.

B **Firm but flexible** wrist.

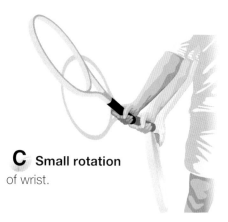

C **Small rotation** of wrist.

D **Large rotation** of wrist.

69

Answer: B

Most novice players will feel comfortable not changing their grip for the backhand and continuing to use their normal forehand grip on the backhand side (Answer A). Unfortunately, although it feels comfortable, it will be a very weak grip when contact is made. This will result in a lack of control and stability of the racket face in the hitting zone. On the forehand, when you make contact, you have the palm of your hand behind the racket on contact, giving you adequate support. However, on the backhand side you have only your fingers and part of your thumb behind the racket on contact, unless you adapt your grip by turning your hand more on top of the racket, which should now place the big knuckle and your thumb firmly behind the grip and behind the ball at contact. At first it will probably feel uncomfortable, but if you persevere with this grip it can make a huge difference to your control and power.

In the standard backhand grip, your hand is turned further over the racket, with your thumb firmly behind the grip.

Answer: B D E

On the single-handed backhand your positioning to the ball is crucial to developing control and power. There are three areas to consider prior to contact:

1. Playing the ball in front of the body and in front of the leading foot enables you to get your body momentum into the shot and significantly reduces any strain on the shot.

2. Playing the ball a comfortable arm's length from the body can help you develop a strong, flowing hit. If you are too close, your swing will be restricted and too gentle. If you are too far away, you will have to overextend your arm and you will lose stability on the swing.

3. Finally, hitting the ball around waist height is a comfortable position that allows your forward swing to start around knee height and finish above shoulder height. It also means the ball is approximately net height already, so you can keep it in court more easily while hitting it quite hard.

The best hitting zones are at waist height, in front of the leading leg, and at an arm's length from the body.

A11

Answer: C

The left hand plays an important role in the single-handed backhand for the right-handed player.

1. It supports the racket in the ready position and enables you to change your grip more easily from forehand to backhand and back again.

2. It supports the racket on take-back, pulling it backward during the backswing and also encouraging the body to rotate, and this creates a long and more efficient take-back.

3. It can be a useful support for players who tend to be a little weak or overflick their wrists during take-back.

4. It can be used by experienced players for power as an opposite force. When the forward swing is reaching the hitting zone, the opposite (left) arm can then be moved backward swiftly so as to increase momentum on the forward swing.

The left hand of a right-handed player plays an important role in the single-handed backhand.

A12

Answer: A B

Using your wrist on a single-handed backhand can aid speed and add spin to your shot. But it can also cause you to lose direction and control. Novice players who are aiming to keep the ball in play should try to keep the wrist firm on contact and through the hitting zone. This should help them control the direction of the racket face at contact, which is crucial for accuracy and consistency. Experienced players who have overcome the first hurdle should now be considering hitting the ball faster and therefore have a firm but flexible wrist to encourage more racket-head speed and slight topspin. Top tournament players try to develop heavy topspin as a tactical weapon, and this requires a considerable amount of wrist movement to "brush up" the ball and create topspin.

A firm but flexible wrist will ensure accuracy and power in the single-handed backhand.

4.4

Topspin

Topspin is created by the angle of the racket's forward swing prior to contact with the ball. This angle makes the ball rotate forward in flight and results in a dipping pattern in the ball's trajectory, as the spin forces the ball downward.

Q13 Many players use topspin when they want to hit the ball hard. What is topspin and why do they feel it will help them play better? Which of the following reasons are correct?

A You can hit the ball **harder.**

B You can **direct** the ball better.

C It is a **less physical** method.

D It gives you a better **margin for error**.

Q14 Established players should generally be able to use a variety of techniques on their ground strokes. This will enable them to adjust their technique to suit a particular game situation. When should you consider using topspin as a tactic?

A When hitting a **hard shot**.

B When hitting an **angled shot**.

C When getting out of **difficulty.**

Topspin swing

Q15 Which of the following technical variations are recognized as helping to develop or improve your topspin technique?

A Swing **low** to high.

B Swing **high** to low.

C Swing as **normal**.

D **Close** racket face at contact.

E **Open** racket face at contact.

F **Brush** up the back of the ball.

Basic forehand swing

Q16 When you are learning to hit with topspin it can be quite difficult to know where to aim the ball, since your swing pattern has now changed from your normal flat shot. What should you do?

A Aim as **normal.**

B Aim **lower** over the net.

C Aim **higher** over the net.

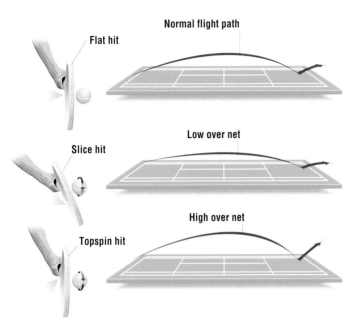

Normal flight path

Flat hit

Low over net

Slice hit

High over net

Topspin hit

Answer: D

The positive effect of using topspin on your ground strokes is the ability to hit the ball aggressively and keep it in play. Topspin gives you a better margin for error over the net. If you hit a normal forehand drive at 60 mph (100kmh) at 3 feet (about 1m) above the net and the ball lands within 3 feet of the baseline, then the same topspin shot would probably make the ball land 15 feet (4.6m) inside the baseline. It therefore follows that, to land the ball near the baseline with a topspin shot, you can afford to hit it higher (say 6 feet, or 1.8m, above the net). This gives you a bigger margin for error and you will hit fewer shots into the net.

A14 Answer: A B

1. Topspin forces the ball downward quickly during flight, enabling players to hit the ball harder, and more safely, than with techniques like slice. It is ideal for the aggressive player.

2. It is an excellent technique to use on a short ball when you are going to hit an angled winner. In this circumstance you probably have only two-thirds of the normal distance to hit the ball, and therefore it is easy to hit the ball out of the court. Aim low over the net and let topspin force the ball downward into the court.

3. It is also an excellent tactic to vary your techniques, using lifted, slice, and topspin, because the flight patterns of these three techniques are significantly varied. An opposing player can be forced into errors simply because he has not judged the shot accurately.

A short crosscourt angled topspin shot will force the ball lower into the court

Answer: A F

When you compare the forward swing of the topspin forehand with the basic lifted forehand, there are some significant technical adjustments to be made. On the topspin shot the following should happen:

1. The forward swing starts lower than normal (about shin height) and finishes above head height.

2. The racket face is vertical at contact and "brushes" up the back of the ball, causing it to rotate forward.

3. The grip is held firmly but is flexible enough to allow the wrist to rotate and impart spin on the ball.

4. The racket head should always be accelerating prior to contact.

5. The elbow should generally finish about shoulder to head height.

6. The body weight should be going into the shot with a significant body rotation after the hit.

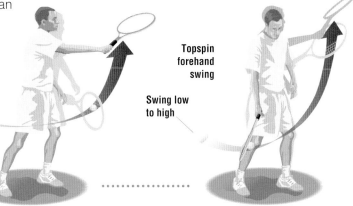

Topspin forehand swing

Swing low to high

Basic forehand swing

Answer: C

Changing your basic swing to incorporate topspin does affect the trajectory of the ball. On a normal lifted shot the forward swing is low to high (about hip to head height), while on a topspin shot the forward swing of the racket head is from very low to very high (about shin height to over head height). Contact with the ball is made with the racket face vertical. This upward swing with a brushing action up the back of the ball causes the forward rotation of the ball, which affects the flight of the ball,

pushing it downward sooner than normal. If you normally hit the ball 4 feet (1.2m) above the net you may now need to aim up to 10 feet (3m) above the net so as to achieve the same aiming point in the opponent's court.

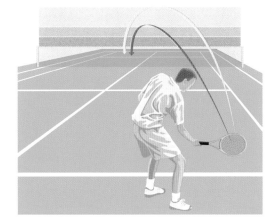

▨ Topspin—aim 10 feet (3m) above net
■ Normal—aim 4 feet (1.2m) above net

Slice

4.5

Slice is created by the angle of the racket's forward swing prior to contact with the ball.
The angle of the racket face has a cutting effect on the bottom edge of the ball, which makes it rotate backward in flight.

Q17 Some players use slice very effectively on their ground strokes, particularly on single-handed backhands. What is the reason for this variation of technique, and which of the following reasons are most applicable?

A You can gain more **control**.

B It's a useful **"rescue"** techique.

C You can hit the ball **harder**.

D It gives you a better **margin for error**.

Q18 Many players consider a slice shot as being weak and defensive, but when you watch world-class players in competition you will often see the slice being used both defensively and aggressively. When should you consider using the slice as a positive tactic?

A On a **high bouncing** ball.

B As a **change of pace**.

C To **attack** the net player.

On a high bouncing ball

As a change of pace

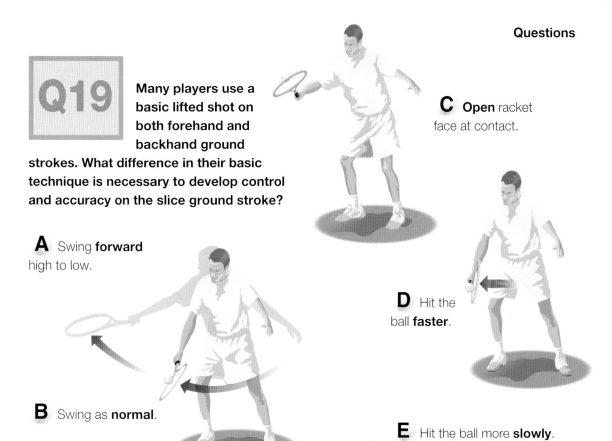

Q19 Many players use a basic lifted shot on both forehand and backhand ground strokes. What difference in their basic technique is necessary to develop control and accuracy on the slice ground stroke?

A Swing **forward** high to low.

B Swing as **normal**.

C **Open** racket face at contact.

D Hit the ball **faster**.

E Hit the ball more **slowly**.

Q20 Because the swing pattern of the racket is now downward on the slice ground stroke, it will affect the direction of the ball unless you adjust your aim. Which of the following is the most likely consideration when using the slice on your ground stroke?

A Aim as **normal**.

B Aim **lower** over the net.

C Aim **higher** over the net.

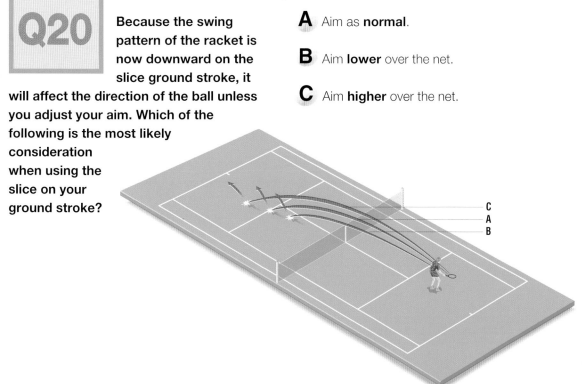

Answer: A B

As a general principle it is not possible to hit a slice ground stroke as hard as topspin and keep it in the court. Some of the main reasons for using a slice are:

1. Because the swing on the slice ground stroke is slower, it is a technique that is designed to aid control and accuracy.

2. The ball "feels" as though it were in contact with the strings longer than a normal shot (3/1,000 second).

3. It is used on all touch shots such as the drop shot, which requires backspin to stop its forward momentum.

4. It is invaluable when you are late for the ball, when your backswing is not prepared early enough, and so your forward swing is late. This is when you can swing downward, open the racket face, drop your bodyweight back and come up with a defensive slice rescue technique to keep the ball in play.

A defensive slice backhand can be used as a "rescue" shot when you are late in hitting the ball.

Answer: A B

Effective slice ground strokes are generally played at medium speed and aimed quite close to the lines. However, it is possible to hit a fast-attacking slice ground stroke if you get the opportunity on a high bouncing ball.

Try to make contact with this ball at chest height with your forward swing going downward from head height to waist height. As this ball is way above net height, you will have given yourself a bigger margin for error and can afford to hit a faster shot with safety. You should also find that your shot (because of the extra backswing) will now bounce lower than normal, which may cause extra concern to your opponent. It is also possible to attack your opponent by varying your (spin) techniques, and also by changing your pace of shot. If your opponent does not notice your swing pattern he may possibly misjudge the bounce of the ball and make an error.

You can hit a fast-attacking slice ground stroke on a high bouncing ball.

Answer: A C E

The slice ground stroke requires three basic changes from the normal lifted techniques:

1. The forward swing needs to start high—at approximately shoulder height—to create a downward swing path.

2. The racket face at contact should be facing slightly upward (open) compared with the usual vertical racket face—this will mean the ball is being hit with backspin.

3. The forward swing momentum is normally slower than that used on either the lifted or topspin shots. This leads to more precise control, which can be very helpful in developing tactical direction.

The slice ground stroke requires a high-to-low forward swing.

Control the angle of the racket face at contact for a successful slice.

Answer: B

The normal forward swing on a lifted shot is low to high (about hip height to head high), whereas the forward swing on a slice shot is high to low. Contact with the ball is made with the racket face slightly open. This downward swing with a "cutting motion" imparts backspin on the ball, which affects its flight path, pushing it upward and possibly out of the court. Aim about 1 foot (0.3m) above the net band to counteract the effect of the spin. However, while you are learning this new skill you could also consider hitting it more slowly and keep your normal aiming point.

4.6

Tactics when **both players are back**

It is not always the better player who wins. An important aspect of play is knowing when to attack or to defend. Your decision should be based upon your position on the court and the strength of your technique. An astute tennis player will search out the opponent's weaknesses while hiding his own.

Q21

When you are playing a competitive singles match it can be quite difficult to know when and where to attack or defend. Are there any golden rules to follow?

A Attack when you feel **positive**.

B Attack from **outside your baseline**.

C Defend when you are **under pressure**.

D Attack the **short ball**.

E Attack the **attacker**.

Q22

When you are under pressure from an opponent's strong deep shot it is often difficult to choose the correct tactical option. What are generally considered to be the most effective options?

C Hit a **drop shot**.

D Hit **hard down the line**.

A
C
D

B

A Hit **high and deep, crosscourt**.

B Hit **crosscourt, short angle**.

Q23 You are about to play a forehand from just inside your baseline and halfway to your sideline. What tactical options are considered most successful in setting up your attack?

A Deep **down the line**.

B Down the middle.

C Crosscourt.

D Drop shot.

E To a **weakness**.

Q24 When your opponent hits a weak short ball you may see that this is your moment to hit a winner, but so often you could end up making mistakes and losing the point. What should you do to overcome this nightmare scenario?

A Hit the ball **very hard**.

B **Watch** the opponent for clues.

C **Aim** near the lines.

D Make your decision **early**.

E **Balance** when you hit.

A21

Answer: C D

Tennis is similar to many sports, with a time to attack but also a time to defend. Experienced players follow the zones-of-court principles to decide which is which:

1. Defense zone. This is the area outside your baseline. From here you should play a safe, deep shot to get yourself out of defense, and to put your opponent on defense.

2. Building zone. This is the area up to 6.5 feet (2m) inside your baseline. If you are playing your shot here you should now be forcing play, trying to create opportunities to set up your next shot for a winner.

3. Attack zone. This is the area from approximately 6.5 feet (2m) inside your baseline up to the service line. If you are hitting shots from here you should be playing winners, but follow to the net just in case your opponent returns them. Note that the above will depend on your reaching the ball early and playing it above hip height; if not, you will need to attack with caution.

■ **Defense zone**
▨ **Building zone**
■ **Attack zone**

A22

Answer: A

Because your opponent has hit a deep shot, you are now in your defense zone and your opponent is hoping for a short and weak return by you, which will give him the opportunity to attack. At this moment the percentage odds must be in favor of your opponent winning the point. Your main task is—hopefully, with one shot—to get out of your defense zone and put yourself on the attack. If you can do this it will completely reverse the odds in your favor. What are the best options?

1. Hit the ball higher over the net than normal; since you are further back in your defense zone this should enable you to hit your shot to land near the opponent's defense zone.

2. Hitting crosscourt means a longer distance than down the line, which can give you more time to recover to a central position on court for your next shot.

Get out of your defense zone and back on the attack with a safe crosscourt.

A high crosscourt return will give you time to recover

Answer: A C E

This is the moment when you can start probing for weaknesses in your opponent's play. You are inside your baseline and you should be putting pressure on your opponent. Try to place your shots to keep her out of the court in her defense zone. It is unlikely that you will hit a winning shot from your building zone but you should be trying to force your opponent to make an error or a weak return, which may give you a chance to play your next shot in your attack zone. Your best options depending on your skill level are:

1. Play deep down the line, giving your opponent less time.

2. Play crosscourt on a short angle forcing the opponent wide out of court.

3. If your opponent has an obvious weakness on one side, play to it to increase the chance of a weak return. However, don't think the point is won yet. Expect the unexpected; with one shot she could put you back into your defense zone!

Playing deep down the line

Answer: D E

When an opponent hits a weak return allowing you to move into your attack zone, it can send a rush of blood to your head as you imagine a marvelous shot you could play from this easy position. Don't be fooled; it looks easy but it isn't. The ball coming toward you:

- has little speed;
- has a trajectory that is different from a normal rallying ball;
- is nearer to the net, giving you only 75 percent of the normal hitting length.

It requires an early decision on:

- whether you are trying to hit a winner or an approach shot;

- where you are going to hit it;
- whether you can get to the ball quickly enough to set up an accurate shot.

From this position you should be able to return most of these easy balls into court, keeping your opponent under pressure, or going for an outright winner. Don't make an unforced error and give the point away when it is almost won.

On a short ball, be aggressive in a controlled manner. Don't go and give the point away!

Net Play

5 When world class players go to the net they usually win the point outright or force their opponent to make an error. Volleying when you are close to the net is fairly easy and generally provides an opportunity to win the point. When you are volleying mid-court, the technique becomes more difficult and you should try to play a shot that enables you to recover to a good net position. To make your volleying more successful you need both a basic technique that is dependable and accurate, and the ability to make quick tactical decisions based upon whether you are in an attacking position or not. Once you have achieved competence in these two areas you should find that going to the net adds a new dimension to your game.

5.1

Approaching the **net**

Approaching the net to play a volley can be a rewarding tactic, especially on a fast court surface. However, on a slow court surface the tactic should be used occasionally, when the point situation is in favor of movement to the net. To be successful, develop your net play to a competent level.

Q1 Many players who are competent at the back of the court feel uncomfortable when they go to the net to volley. What are the advantages of approaching the net during a point?

A You give your opponent **less time**.

B You could win the point **quickly**.

C You use **less energy**.

D You can create **more angles**.

More angles of play are available from the net

Q2 In a singles match, deciding when to move to the net to attack can be a difficult decision for a player to make. Are there any principles to help you make the right decision?

A When you need a **breather**.

B When hitting a ground stroke **on your baseline**.

C When you have developed a sound **basic volley**.

D When you are attacking **well inside** your baseline.

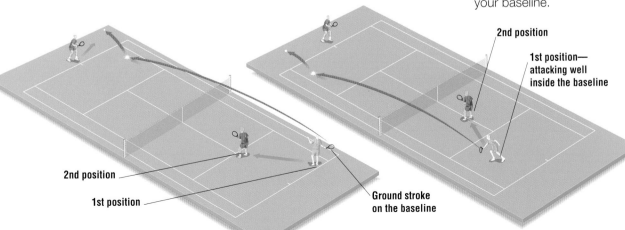

2nd position

1st position—attacking well inside the baseline

2nd position

1st position

Ground stroke on the baseline

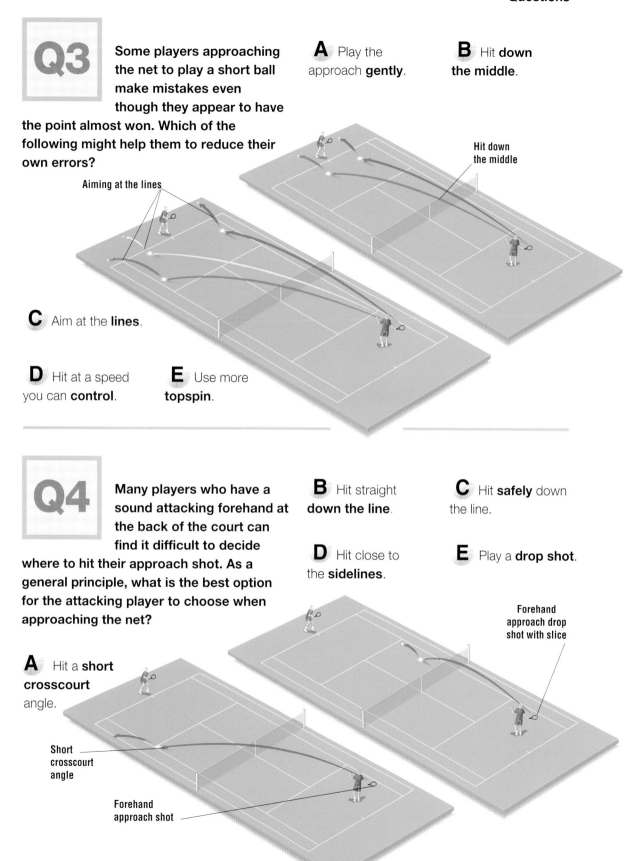

Q3 Some players approaching the net to play a short ball make mistakes even though they appear to have the point almost won. Which of the following might help them to reduce their own errors?

A Play the approach **gently**.

B Hit **down the middle**.

Hit down the middle

Aiming at the lines

C Aim at the **lines**.

D Hit at a speed you can **control**.

E Use more **topspin**.

Q4 Many players who have a sound attacking forehand at the back of the court can find it difficult to decide where to hit their approach shot. As a general principle, what is the best option for the attacking player to choose when approaching the net?

B Hit straight **down the line**.

C Hit **safely** down the line.

D Hit close to the **sidelines**.

E Play a **drop shot**.

Forehand approach drop shot with slice

A Hit a **short crosscourt** angle.

Short crosscourt angle

Forehand approach shot

Answer: A D

If you go to the net to volley you have immediately reduced the distance between you and your opponent by almost 50 percent. This will mean that when you play a volley your opponent at the back of the court will have far less time to prepare her shot. The tactic can force opponents into making errors on their passing shots. (However, it can also rebound on you because you now have less time to prepare your own shots!) Another consideration is that the nearer to the net you are, the more opportunity you have to create angles with your return and make your opponent run further to return your volley.

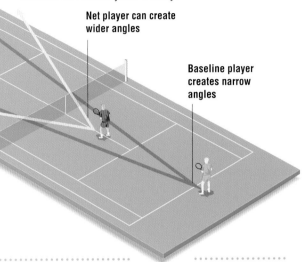

Net player can create wider angles

Baseline player creates narrow angles

Answer: C D

It is no use going to the net in matches if you are very weak on the volley and lose most of your points there. If this is the case you need to practice your volley to develop basic techniques and skills. You should then create drills that replicate a match situation. Practice will build your confidence in this area of your game and help you to become an all-court player. As a general principle, you would approach the net on a short ball (weak shot) from your opponent. If you can play your baseline shot from well inside your baseline, approximately halfway between the service line and the baseline, you should be able to set up a strong position on court for your next shot—a volley.

Practice will build your confidence and help you develop basic volleying techniques and skills.

Answer: D E

When many players get a short ball and see the opportunity to set up an attack, they try to hit a little harder than normal and make mistakes. Remember, when you hit an approach shot you are further up the court than usual, which gives your opponent less time to prepare, so resist the urge to try to speed up your shot. Because you are now closer to your opponent and hitting a shorter distance, there is a tendency to overhit out of court.

If you hit such a shot at your normal speed and height over the net, you will need to use more topspin to develop a bigger margin of safety and keep it in play.

You can calculate the mathematics of playing a short ball.

78 feet (24m)
68 feet (21m)
60 feet (18m)
50 feet (15m)

Answer: A C

An approach shot should make the opponent run and give him less time to play his shots. The two favored shots are **(1)** down the line, and **(2)** short-angle crosscourt.

1st position—in ready position

2nd position—needs to run to get ball back

A down-the-line approach shot gives the opponent less time.

The down-the-line approach gives the opponent less time and fewer angles to play against the volleyer, and should set up the volleyer with an attacking position for his next shot.

A short-angle approach (winner) can be used when the ball can be played at approximately net height. This shot, generally played with topspin, creates a huge angle and forces the opponent wide and out of court.

Your decision will depend on the old trade-off—which is your best shot, and what are your opponent's weaknesses?

5.2

Volleying
techniques

Net play is generally considered to be one of the main attacking positions in tennis play. It can be very rewarding to hit winning volleys and finish the point quickly in your favor.

Q6 When you are at the net and in a good position, it can be very frustrating to still make a mistake with a ball played at medium speed and net height. Which of the following can help your technique?

A Take a **backswing** for more control.

B **Reduce** the backswing for more control.

C **Follow through** in the direction of your shot.

D Contact the ball in front of your **leading hip**.

E Contact the ball in front of your **leading foot**.

Q5 When intermediate players are moving to the net, what are the important basic principles to consider for the approach-and-volley tactic?

A Get to the net as **quickly** as possible.

B Try to set up a **balanced hitting position**.

C Go for a winner on the **approach shot**.

D **Be prepared** for your opponent's next shot.

E Make your **first volley** a winner.

Q7 Playing a volley below net height will require some variation of your basic volleying technique. Which of the following might apply?

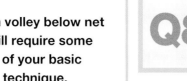 **Q8** Determining which grip to use on the volley can be quite a difficult decision for intermediate players who are playing doubles and are involved in quick-volleying rallies. Which of the following grips might be considered most appropriate?

A Contact the ball level with your **front hip**.

B Contact the ball level with your **front foot**.

A **Forehand** grip on all volleys.

C Contact the ball **well in front of** your front foot.

B **Backhand** grip on all volleys.

C **Change** to the appropriate grip.

D **Drop your wrist** to slice the ball up.

E Keep your body **low and balanced**.

D **Halfway** grip between A and B on all volleys.

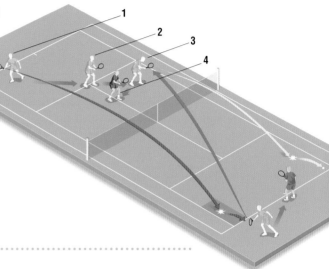

A5

Answer: B D

When moving to the net you need to set up a balanced hitting position for your first volley. You have to move as quickly as you can to the net, but you must set up a ready position as well. When and how do you do this? Imagine you are approaching the net. Just as your opponent is about to make contact with the ball you should stop moving forward and, using a split step, get into a ready position that will enable you to move in any direction in a balanced and controlled manner. Many players fail in this area because they don't check their forward movement, and that leads to a poorly constructed volley.

Having played your first volley, try to gain a strong attacking position at the net by repeating the previous process of **(1)** hit your shot, **(2)** check into ready position, **(3)** play your next shot, and **(4)** recover to a central ready position.

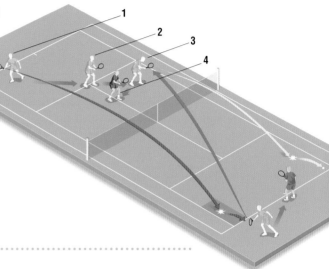

A6

Answer: B E

The art of volleying is best summed up in the phrase "the less you do, the better it will be." Most players who make mistakes volleying appear to play a similar swing to their groundstrokes. The problem is they have less time to prepare, and less distance to hit than when playing from the baseline. In most volleys the ball is coming toward you quite quickly, so all you really need to do is to put the racket in the way (like a brick wall) and set the racket face at an appropriate angle. The ball will almost certainly go back into play. If you want to send it back harder than it came, set up a strong body position, taking a very small backswing (approximately 1 foot, or 0.3m) and accelerate the racket head forward (similar to a sharp forward punch), contacting the ball in front of your leading foot. This should be all you need for a powerful volley.

In volleying, keep racket movements short and simple to ensure success.

Answer: C E

Volleys are generally considered to be attacking shots played from an attacking position near the net. However, when you are forced to play a volley from below net height you are generally in a semidefensive position and will need to play carefully rather than go for a winner. Slight changes in technique are caused by the height

of the ball when you make contact. Because it is a low shot you need to bend your knees for balance and make contact with the ball well in front of your leading foot (further forward than normal). This should allow the racket face's angle to open up naturally, which will mean that more volleys will go over the net (and hopefully land in court).

Low volleys must be played from a balanced position.

Answer: D

In the early stages of learning volleying, most players find it easier to use the same grip as for their ground strokes. This is quite natural and is a good starting point, but it has limitations, especially if players have extreme grips on forehand or backhand. As players improve, the game becomes faster and they have less time to change their grip when they are volleying close to the net and their opponents come into volley at the same time. This is where one grip becomes preferable. As a general guide, try to develop a volley grip that is halfway between

your forehand and single-handed backhand grips. This grip is commonly called a "continental grip."

More established players can use the halfway grip known as "continental" for volleying.

Net play **variations**

5.3

At the net you may meet with a variety of opportunities to create a winning situation. You will need to add to your basic volleying techniques in order to control the point from the net. Some of these shots are played infrequently but will require practice if you want to make your net play successful.

Q9 One of the more difficult volley situations is when you are moving into the net and are forced to play a low volley (below net height) from just inside your service line. Which of the following pointers could help you improve in this tricky area of the court?

A Aim the ball near the **lines**.

B Use more **wrist** than on the normal volley.

C Keep **moving quickly** to the net.

D Aim your shot **deep**.

E Try to set up a **balanced hitting position**.

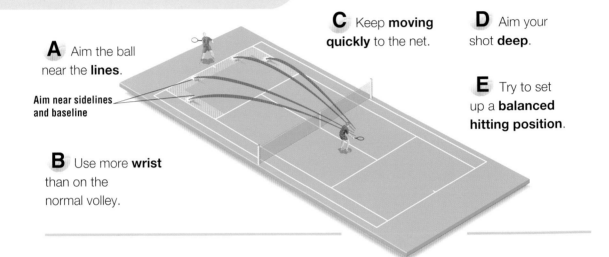

Aim near sidelines and baseline

Q10 When you watch top players at the net, you will sometimes see them play a shot known as the "drive volley." When should they play the shot, and what are some technical changes they might make?

A On a **high, slow** ball.

B On a **low** ball.

C On a **fast** ball

D On a **slow** ball.

E Hit a normal volley **faster**.

F Take a **backswing**.

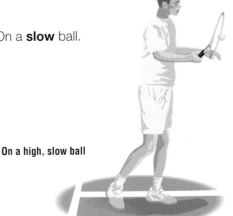

On a low ball

On a high, slow ball

Q11

When top players volley, it appears they can change the direction and angle of their volley without appearing to do anything different. Which of the following possible answers gives the best clue to developing this skill?

B Use more **wrist**.

C Change the **position** of your body.

D Contact the ball **further forward** for crosscourt.

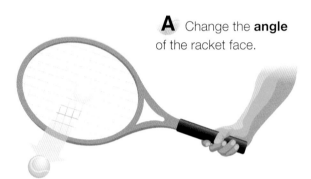

A Change the **angle** of the racket face.

E Use **topspin**.

Q12

The smash can be considered one of the most satisfying shots to play, when performed well. However, many players have extreme difficulty in even bringing their smashes into play. What pointers might help to improve this aspect of your game?

A Don't be afraid to **attack** the ball.

B Try to aim for the **line**.

C Try to set up a **sound hitting position**.

D **Jump** for your smash.

E Try to develop a **smooth throwing action**.

F Use more **wrist** than normal.

Answer: D E

Playing a low first volley just inside your service line is usually considered to be a very demanding shot. Two basic principles need to be considered. The first one is that it is extremely difficult to hit a fast volley into the court. Also, the percentages are well against your hitting a winning shot. So what's the answer? You need to play a very accurate shot to get you out of defense and onto the attack. You need to hit your volley as deep as you can near to the opponent's baseline (within 6.5 feet, or 2m). This will force her to play her next shot from behind her baseline,

which is considered to be a very defensive position. To do this requires a steady, balanced hitting position when you make contact with the ball—stepping forward to play the ball well in front of your leading foot with the knees comfortably flexed.

In this situation, try to play the ball early.

Answer: A F

This is a rewarding shot to play well. You are now really on the attack. The ball coming to you is slow, high, and easy to hit. Try to imagine it is similar to a shoulder-high ground stroke played from the back of the court. The one major difference is that you have a much shorter distance to hit the ball, so you need to aim it lower over the net with the trajectory of your forward swing aiming slightly downward, as opposed to upward from the back of the court.

A drive volley played off a slow, high ball.

The direction of the ball is dependent on the angle of the racket face.

A11

Answer: A D

Changing direction on the volley from straight to crosscourt is in theory incredibly simple. A basic point to remember is that the ball always goes in the direction the racket faces at contact. Therefore, to change direction you need to "set" the angle of the racket so that it points in the right direction. This is similar to when you play against a brick wall; the ball will always rebound back. If you were to change the angle of the brick wall, the ball would go in another direction.

A12

Answer: C E

World-class players nearly always win the point when they play a smash, and make it look easy. What can we learn from them to help us to develop smashing skills? Try to visualize your smash as being similar to a serve, but imagine that you have tossed the ball into an awkward position, some distance away from you. You need to get into a strong serve position to attack the ball. This requires **(1)** watching the ball carefully, **(2)** judging where you need to move to, **(3)** movement and adjustment of your footwork, and **(4)** copying your serve throwing action as closely as you can. A golden rule to help you smash better is: "Try to keep the ball in front of you; don't let it get behind you."

A sound hitting position is paramount when playing a smash.

5.4 Opponent approaching the net

This is generally the time when your opponent is on the attack and you are trying to defend or possibly counterattack. The two main options will be either a passing shot or a lob, depending on the tactical situation and your level of skill.

Q13

As an intermediate player, when your opponent is moving in to the net, you may often find it difficult to choose your shot. Do you go for a passing shot, or should you lob? Which of the following would point you toward a probable passing shot?

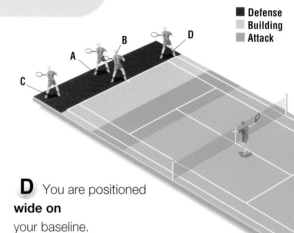

■ Defense
■ Building
■ Attack

A You are positioned **outside** your baseline.

B You are positioned **on** your baseline.

C You are positioned **wide outside** your baseline.

D You are positioned **wide on** your baseline.

Q14

Your opponent is moving in to the net after an approach shot. However, he has hit it short on your backhand side and you now have the opportunity to hit a passing shot. What are your best options?

A Aim **close to the inside** of the sidelines.

B Aim about **3 feet (1m) inside** the sidelines.

C Aim about **5 feet (1.5m) inside** the sidelines.

D Aim to hit the **service line**.

E Aim about 3 feet (1m) inside the **baseline**.

Q15

What are the technical changes necessary to hit a passing shot successfully, either for an outright winner or to force a weak reply from your opponent?

D Hit as **normal**.

E Aim **lower** over the net.

A Hit a **faster**-than-normal shot.

B Use the **slice**.

C Use more **topspin**.

Q16

When you are going to hit a forehand lob as a defensive reply, what are the changes you should consider to your normal forehand ground-stroke technique?

Using a shorter swing

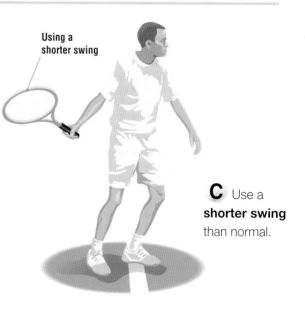

A Swing forward from **very low** to **very high**.

C Use a **shorter swing** than normal.

B **Open** the racket face by using more wrist.

D Hit it **softer** than normal.

E Hit it **harder** than normal.

player   opponent

A13

Answer: B D

There are no firm rules about when to play a passing shot or a lob against an opponent who is moving into the net. It depends on your personal skills and confidence level on either shot, as well as your position on court when you are planning your shot. Here are three things to bear in mind:

As a general rule, if you are inside your baseline, you should mainly hit passing shots and topspin attacking lobs.

If you are outside your baseline you should mainly hit a variety of lobs with occasional passing shots.

If you are on the baseline it becomes a choice between the first two. Remember also your own forehand and backhand strengths and weaknesses, because these will affect your decision-making.

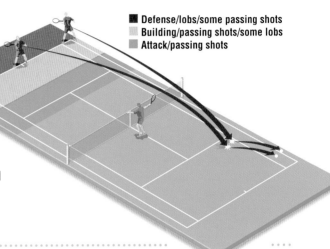

■ Defense/lobs/some passing shots
▨ Building/passing shots/some lobs
▢ Attack/passing shots

A14

Answer: B D

When your opponent has decided to move to the net but has hit a short ball, this is definitely your chance to hit a winning passing shot. The down-the-line pass is the most awkward for the volleyer. It is the shortest distance; it will pull the volleyer away from a center-ready position and give only one angle to play. You should aim for your shot to hit the service line, which could force your opponent to play a difficult low volley if he can reach it. You should aim approximately 3–5 feet (1–1.5m) inside the sideline to make sure your ball goes in court. As you become more confident try angles nearer to the lines, but don't overdo it and make errors from what should be a winning position.

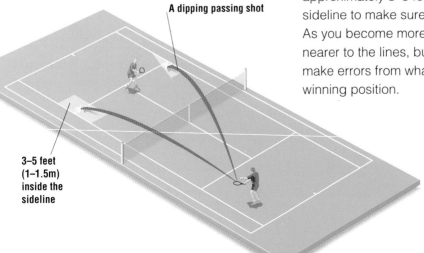

A dipping passing shot

3–5 feet (1–1.5m) inside the sideline

Answer: B C E

To be successful in passing an opponent at the net, you need a combination of speed and accuracy. This is known as the power-control trade-off. You know the most difficult volleys are those below net height, so how can you force this on an opponent? You need the ball to travel quickly over the net and then dip below net height before the opponent plays her volley. Aim the

ball quite low over the net—about a foot (0.3m), and put quite a heavy topspin on the ball, forcing it downward. This will require a faster "brushing action" up the ball to ensure it is already dipping downward as it passes the net. An alternative and less aggressive method is to chop (slice) the ball delicately so that it creates a similar but slower effect.

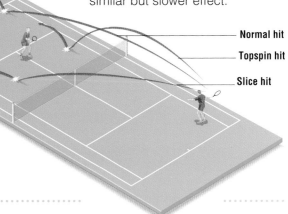

Normal hit
Topspin hit
Slice hit

Answer: A D

When you play a basic forehand lob without spin from a defensive position, you must make some changes to your normal ground-stroke technique. You now need the ball to clear the opponent's reach by at least 3 feet (about 1m). With the highest point on your lob arcing between the opponent's volleying position and his service line, you need **(1)** to set the lowest part of the backswing far lower than usual, **(2)** to swing your racket upward on a sharper climb than usual, and **(3)** to finish your forward swing high above your head. You will also need to hit the ball more softly than your normal forehand drive.

To lob successfully, swing your racket from very low to very high.

Shot selection

5.5

When your opponent moves in to the net to attack, you will be put under physical and mental pressure. There are a number of possible shots to play, but which is the best counterattacking or defending option? Making a successful passing shot or lob will require an alert mind and quick decision-making.

Q17

Occasionally, you see high-level players hitting a winning topspin lob from an attacking position in their court. What changes are necessary in their normal technique to hit the ball over their opponents' heads but still keep it inside the baseline?

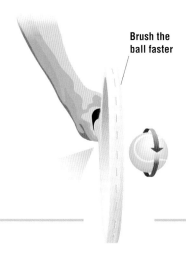

Brush the ball faster

A Hit the ball **harder**.

B "**Brush**" the ball faster.

C Aim **lower** over the opponent.

D Use more **wrist**.

Q18

Many players are told to use only the down-the-line passing shot because it is the shortest distance and gives the net player less time. However, under what circumstances could a crosscourt passing shot be a sound option?

D When you are **outside your baseline**.

E When you are **outside your sideline**.

When you are outside your baseline

A As a **change of tactic**.

B When the **opponent is slow** moving to the net.

When the opponent is at the net

C When the opponent is **at the net**.

Q19 When your opponent is moving in to hit an attacking shot from well inside her court, it is very difficult to know where her shot is going to land. What can you do to help yourself quickly reach her attacking shot?

A **Bend** your knees more.

B Take **little steps**.

C Take **big steps**.

D **Sprint** when you see the direction.

E Anticipate direction and **move early**.

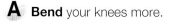

Q20 Watching club players play passing shots, you quite often see a situation where the volleyer manages to "scramble" back the attempted pass. Often the player is not expecting the ball to come back and then makes a mistake with an easy opportunity to win the point. What should you do in this same situation?

A Expect the ball to **come back**.

B **Follow your pass** to the net.

C Have a **follow-up shot** planned.

D Hit your follow-up shot **down the line**.

E Hit your follow-up shot **crosscourt**.

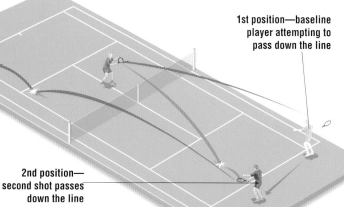

1st position—baseline player attempting to pass down the line

2nd position— second shot passes down the line

Answer: A B D

The attacking topspin lob can be one of the most exciting and rewarding shots to play. You will need the ability to play sound topspin forehands from the back of the court as a foundation for this great shot. The topspin lob requires some basic adaptations to a normal topspin shot from the back of the court. You will need to get the ball spinning much faster than

normal. To achieve this you should drop the racket head very low on full take-back and then accelerate the forward swing so as to achieve fast ball rotation. The racket head accelerates on impact; you will need to let the wrist rotate at speed after the hit, with the elbow finishing higher than the wrist at the end of the shot.

A topspin lob requires a steep swing with a fast brushing action.

Answer: A B

The crosscourt passing shot is generally the easier pass for the volleyer to intercept, so the down-the-line pass is overall the best

percentage option. However, when you have hit a few down-the-line passing shots your opponent will probably be expecting another to go down the line. Now is the time for a change of tactic and to bring in a crosscourt variation. This can force the volleyer into uncertainty and so being late in preparing subsequent volleys. The other obvious time to play crosscourts is when the opponent is slow moving in, and is nearer the service line than the net. This leaves a big gap to play into across the front of the attacker who has failed to get close to the net.

A successful crosscourt pass

Don't be predictable. Vary the pattern of your passing shots.

Don't wait for things to happen—make them happen. Move early.

A19

Answer: E

In this situation the attacker appears to be in a strong winning situation. The odds are she is going to hit with speed, whether crosscourt or down the line. If you wait till the ball is hit you will be too late—you must make an educated guess. The timing of your move is vitally important, so make up your mind early which way you will go, but don't move until your opponent is on the forward swing of her shot just prior to hitting the ball. This should give you a little extra time in setting up your next shot.

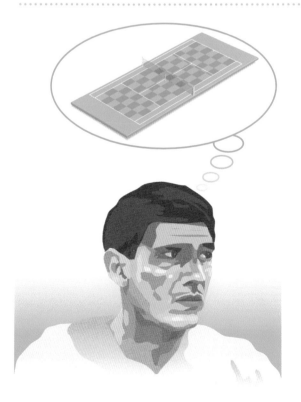

A20

Answer: A C

When you play a passing shot you should always anticipate that your opponent might get it back, so be alert and on your toes, and be ready to move in any direction. Also try to anticipate where the opponent might play his volley and have your next shot planned in the back of your mind. Tennis is not a one-shot game. Try to notice the patterns of play in different areas of court. If you can have advance warning of your opponent's intentions, it will make your life much easier on court.

Tennis is not a one-shot game. It is chess on the move!

Elements of the Game

6 Mental and physical skills and regular practice are all fundamental to the success of any player. Top tennis players are supremely fit athletes, with a strong mental approach to the highs and lows of competition, and they achieve their level of success with a planned, dedicated regime. To play tennis well you will need the four physical "S"s—speed, suppleness, strength, and stamina—as well as the four mental "C"s—commitment, control, concentration, and confidence. And remember two mottos: "Practice makes perfect" and "The more I practice, the luckier I get!"

Mental skills

6.1

To play sport well you need to enjoy the ups and downs of competition. There will be times when you are enjoying yourself and feeling positive, and other times when you will be feeling disappointed and negative. How you learn to control your emotional state is a major key to success on a tennis court.

Q2

At all levels of play, from beginner to world class, confidence is a major factor. You often see players playing well for a period of time, and then appearing to go "off their game" and make mistakes. What can you do to prevent this situation from arising, or, if it does, how can you overcome it?

A Expect to win every match.

B Expect to win every point.

C Try to hit winners.

D Play **within your capabilities**.

E Try to cut out **unforced errors**.

F Have a **game plan**.

Q1

When you watch the world's top players in competition, they appear to be very different in their attitudes and the way they play their matches. However they play, they appear to be successful even when they have very different personalities. How can you develop a game style and positive attitude to competitive play?

A Play the game the way **you** would like to play.

B Choose a **top player** and copy him or her.

C Model your game on a top player of **similar physique**.

D Keep **changing** your game style.

Q3 In most tennis matches more than 75 percent of the time is used between points and changes of ends. There is a large amount of time when you are not playing a point but thinking about the last point, the next point, and so on. This is when you can lose concentration, which can affect your performance. What can you do to stop this from happening?

A **Analyze** the last point.

B **Study your opponent** carefully for any clues.

C **Mentally relax** and look away from the court.

D **Focus** your eyes on the strings of your racket.

E **Plan** your next point.

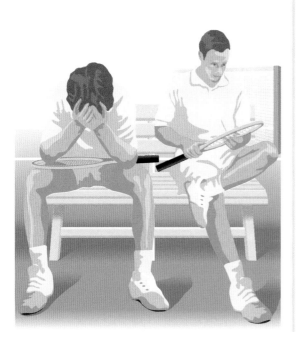

Q4 Many players react very differently during matches. Some appear cool and controlled no matter what the situation, while others appear to be living on an emotional tightrope and seem angry and frustrated. What should you do to improve this area of your game?

A **Try not to show** any emotion.

B **Show your feelings** most of the time.

C Be true to your emotions—**be natural**.

D Try to **"pump" yourself up**.

E Be natural but **retain your self-control**.

Answer: A

People play sports for many reasons, and it is the same with tennis. All players uniquely bring to their sport dreams, values, and aspirations all wrapped in individual personalities and physiques. Tennis players should be true to their own personality and values when they step on the court. If you are very careful in life you will probably be the same on the court—hardly taking

chances, keeping the ball in play, and trying to force the opponent into mistakes. If you are a great gambler in life this will probably reflect in your tennis, because you will try to go for winning shots when the odds are not always in your favor. Between these two personality types are a myriad of others. Think about your philosophy of sport and why you play tennis, and try to be true to your personal values. It is very useful to watch top players but you are more likely to improve your own game if you take elements of their game and adapt it to your own, rather than try to copy their style.

Answer: D F

The saying "competence breeds confidence" is very true. How can we make this relevant to tennis players? You need to have a broad picture of what you are capable of doing successfully, both tactically and

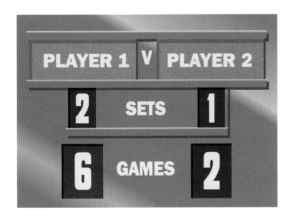

technically. You should then identify a game plan that suits your style of play, and try to use it in your match. You should now try to play within your capabilities regardless of the standard of your opponent. This can be very difficult against a better opponent, as the ball keeps coming back and pushes you up to the edge of your capabilities. Remember, there is no disgrace in losing to a better player; it is how you manage the situation that is important. Goal setting can be a major factor. If you have always lost to a certain player 6–2, 6–2, set yourself a goal of winning six games in the next match. This will set you a realistic goal to achieve. Copy athletes and set yourself realistic "personal bests" to build your self-confidence.

Answer: D E

"Concentration" is a key word in tennis, but what does it mean? It is the ability to focus on the necessary factors that will aid performance, and to discard other factors that are not relevant. So what should you concentrate on between points?

Here are some suggestions:

- You must go on court with an overall game plan and some individual tactical situation you are going to use when you are serving and receiving.
- After the point, do not dwell on mistakes you have just made.
- Try to relax for a few seconds with good breathing techniques.
- Think about the next point and any tactics you want to use.
- Look at the strings on your racket while you are thinking to stop your eyes and mind from wandering elsewhere.
- Make up your mind and go into the next point with a positive approach to what you are about to do, and try to implement it.

Answer: E

Again, your personality and attitude are the key to this area and you will need to let your emotions come out; but they should not be excessive and outside the rules of the game. If you are an excitable person, it would be wrong to show no emotion, because you will feel restricted and frustrated. Conversely, if you are a quiet, shy, retiring person, it would probably feel silly and exhibitionist to go around giving highfives. In each case, you need to be aware of your emotional state, with some players needing to calm down a little while others need a little more adrenaline and lift. The main aim is to perform efficiently, by not allowing yourself to lose self-control and trying to think positively about the point in hand and the next point. Remember, tennis is not a personal war between two factions; it is a sporting competition. Enjoy the challenge. Losing is not a disgrace; it is part of learning.

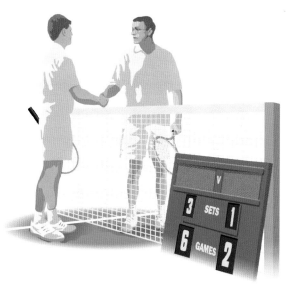

Physical skills

6.2

Tennis is an explosive game. Most points comprise three to six shots, equaling five to fifteen seconds of dynamic action. The physical skills required include speed, strength, stamina, suppleness, and a high level of coordination. There is a great deal of truth in the phrase "athlete first, tennis player second."

Q6 A tennis match is not played in a specified amount of time, as many sports are. A three-set match could be finished within thirty minutes or three hours, especially in tournaments, where you could play two or even three matches a day. What can you do as a player to develop your stamina for this possibility?

Q5 One of the challenges in tennis is to be quick around the court, not just to reach the ball but also to recover quickly for your opponent's next shot. Often you see players who are quick to the first shot but are always struggling to set up good positions for their subsequent shots. What factors do they need in order to overcome this problem?

A They need to **use their legs** more efficiently.

B Run **faster** after the shot.

Running fast after the ball

C Concentrate on their balance.

D Run with **shorter steps**.

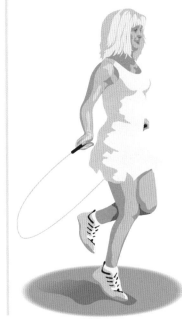

A Rely on your **natural fitness**.

B Devise a personal **training schedule**.

C Train every day in the gym on **exercise bikes**.

D Train with **six-mile (ten-km)** runs.

Q7 One of the most fascinating aspects of tennis is the variety of shots that you can play during a match. Each shot has a unique combination of movements, and requires coordination, timing, and agility to achieve success. Probably one of the most difficult skills is to position your body effectively to perform a particular technique. Which footwork pattern might help you achieve a sound "hitting zone"?

A Take **short steps** to the ball.

B Take **long steps** to the ball.

C Take a **mixture** of A and B.

D Take **long steps, then short steps.**

E Take **long steps, then adjusting steps.**

Taking long steps to the ball

Q8 In the modern world of tennis, strength appears to be an important factor in the development of players. If you want to improve your game with a strength-training program, what are the factors you need to consider?

A Lightweight, **low** repetition.

B Heavyweight, **high** repetition.

C Refer to **expert** advice.

D Lightweight, **high** repetition.

Answer: A

When you watch top tennis players run to play ground strokes, you will notice that they generally sprint to where the ball is going. They do some positioning steps around the ball, then hit their shot so that the finish of the shot becomes the start of their recovery to a central ready position.

This is a fluid motion that requires the shot to be hit in a balanced manner, allowing fast recovery for a subsequent shot. The legs and knees are the key to balance and recovery. A good practice is the "fan" drill. Place six balls in different positions around the court. The job is to run to pick up one ball, bring it back to the baseline, and then pick up the next ball until all six balls are at the baseline. Time yourself with a stopwatch and then try to improve your time.

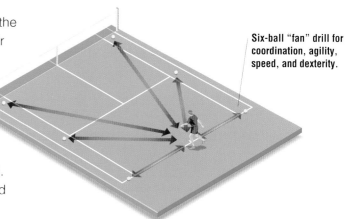

Six-ball "fan" drill for coordination, agility, speed, and dexterity.

Answer: B

A tennis player needs great stamina in order to continue performing to his optimum level when he has already played for a period of time in a possibly long match.

Players will use energy in short bursts during a match, and this will gradually reduce their efficiency over a period of time. It is not as noticeable as with athletes, who run against the clock, but it is a major factor in being an effective tennis player. Every tennis player is different in his physical makeup so you need specific advice about your strengths and weaknesses. Because of this you need a personal training schedule that is tailor-made for your requirements. Why not seek advice from a professional? Try your nearest gym and ask for advice and a personal plan from a personal trainer who knows the physical demands of tennis.

Tennis may make you fitter, but you need to get fit for tennis first!

Answer: E

As a general rule, you need to take long steps, then adjusting steps to achieve a sound hitting zone. The aim is to reach the ball as quickly as possible, hence the long steps, and then have time to make fine-tuning smaller steps prior to your shot. There are always exceptions. For example, when the ball comes straight back to you, you will not require the long steps, but only the adjusting steps. The key to developing agility is to practice quick, small movements of the feet, which will increase your speed around the ball. Then it comes down to your ability to judge the speed and flight of the ball, and to put your body in the optimum position for your intended shot. Two very good exercises for developing agility are:

- Skipping while varying your footwork patterns.
- Running around cones forward, backward, sideways, or a combination of all three.

Answer: C D

To be a good tennis player you will require upper-body and lower-body strength, but you do not require the build of a weight lifter! You need strength but you must have muscle speed in order to move swiftly and to swing the racket head quickly on a fast shot. It is commonly known as the strength–speed trade-off, and once again it depends on your personal physique. If you find your legs are getting tired, or your arm is weak or aching after a couple of sets, you could be a prime candidate for a personal program of strength training in the appropriate areas (with light weights and high repetitions). First, though, do seek the advice of a personal trainer, who will evaluate your needs professionally and can then set an appropriate training schedule for you.

Strength training should be supervised by a professional trainer.

How to **practice**

6.3

If you want to improve, you need to practice regularly. Playing matches is only part of the process. Identify your strengths and weaknesses, then prioritize areas to work on, and set yourself some practice goals. With regular practice you will be amazed at your improvement. Don't talk about it, do it!

Q10

How should you structure a practice session to improve your technique, and so take your game to a higher level?

A A technique in **isolation**.

Q9

Many players find it difficult to improve their game because of lack of practice opportunities. If you fit into this category, what standard of practice partner could help you best?

A A **better** player.

B A **lesser** player.

C A player of the **same standard**.

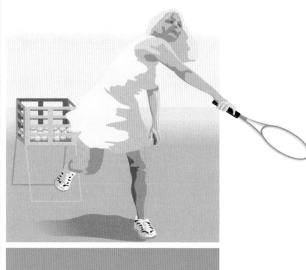

B A technique in a **game-related** situation.

C A technique in **competition**.

Q11 Many successful club-standard players play to a set game plan, which, although it works well, lacks variety and can be predictable. What should they do to try to add another dimension to their game?

A Play a **variety** of opponents.

B Identify a strategy and **drill** it.

C Experiment with new strategies in **match play**.

D Experiment with new strategies **in practice**.

Q12 When you are starting tennis it is often difficult to find a willing practice partner of the same standard who can make improving your game a challenging task. This is where a practice wall is a fantastic aid to give you regular practice opportunities. What are the advantages of hitting against a wall to develop your technique?

A The ball will **always come back**.

B The ball will have **little spin.**

C You quickly know **where it is going**.

D You can design **tactical training** situations.

Answer: C

The correct practice environment is one where you can develop your skills and tactics in a planned and methodical manner. You need adequate court time with a practice partner who can help you improve various aspects of your game. If your partner is a few standards below or well above your playing standard, it will be hard to set the appropriate tempo and speed in your drills. Everyone wants to play against someone better to acclimatize to a stronger, faster game, but it is not the best way to learn a new skill. You need to find a partner who wants to work out with you in a cooperative manner so that you can both improve your games. Take turns with one player practicing a skill, while a practice partner sets up drills and exercises and gives realistic feedback, and then change over. Remember, practice makes perfect—but perfect practice makes your skills more perfect.

Answer: B

Intermediate-level players will often find that the next level of improvement requires variations to basic techniques and the acquisition of new tactics:

1. When first trying a new technique you may need to hit a particular shot in isolation repetitively just to get a feel for it.

2. However, as soon as possible you need to set up a simulated game-play situation appropriate to when and where that shot might be used. You need to practice the technique frequently in this situation to develop tactical awareness.

3. You need to create this tactical situation in a practice match in an open-play situation to see if the technique can still work.

This last practice situation incorporates anticipation and decision making, which underpin any tactical shot making. If you practice only in situations 1 and 2, you will become proficient in practice but unable to replicate this in match play.

You will improve by building your practice logically and gradually.

Answer: B D

There are two key questions to ask yourself if you want to improve your tactical play: **(1)** Which tactic do I use that could be improved? **(2)** Which tactic would I

like to add to my game? For example, you may wish to develop a serve–volley tactic for surprise in singles and regular use in doubles play.

- You need an appropriate partner to help you achieve the feel of this tactic.
- Don't play points yet, set up a routine in which you drill the serve–volley tactic repetitively. At this stage, your practice partner should return most serves to you so that you get the feel of the first volley.
- Next, begin to make the drill more authentic by having your partner vary the returns.
- Finally, play practice points.

It is all a question of laying solid foundations—building a skill to achieve a tactic that will be of value in a match.

Answer: A D

Finding a practice partner can often be difficult, so why not try to find a court or club that has a rebound wall to practice against.

The beauty of playing against a wall is that you can be as selfish as you like. You can practice what you want, when you want, and how you want, without one murmur of complaint. If you are learning a new technique, all you need to improve are a few balls, an inquiring mind, a competitive urge, and patience. With a new technique, try to develop the skill, the shape of

swing and so on, by hitting slow and short rallies against the wall. As you begin to improve, concentrate on retaining your technique when you are hitting a little harder from a greater distance. At this stage don't worry about mistakes—they are good for the learning experience. The wall is a very experienced player. What more do you want? The ball will always come back.

A wall is the most uncomplaining practice partner you will ever find!

Equipment

This section is to give you some thoughts on the equipment you may require if you are starting to play tennis. You should, however, try to discuss equipment with friends who already play tennis or similar sports, and then talk to sports stores specializing in tennis, or, probably best of all, to a tennis pro at your club, who should be able not only to advise you but also let you test some rackets from a demonstration range.

RACKETS

You need to be comfortable with the feel of a racket. It should not be too heavy or the grip too large. Don't spend too much money on your first racket, since you will probably want to upgrade it once you become more proficient. Children's rackets are smaller and lighter, according to the size of the player. Never buy a racket for a child thinking "she'll grow into it"; by the time this happens she may have grown out of tennis because of lack of success!

SHOES

You need tennis shoes that are designed for the varied movement patterns and court surfaces you may encounter. Remember, tennis is a sport that requires fast, explosive movement allied to agility, for all those small adjusting steps you often need to make around the ball. Before you buy your shoes, try to identify the type of court surface you will usually be playing on.

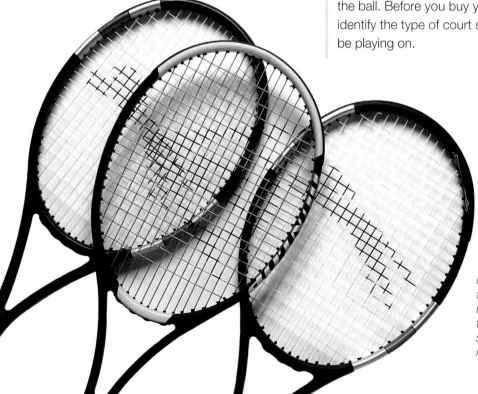

It is worth taking the time to study the market and find the racket that is right for you. If possible, try to test-play your racket first. Many sports shops will let you try out a racket before you purchase.

CLOTHING

There is a huge range of tennis clothing now available on the market. If you know where you are going to play, check out the accepted form of clothing, which may guide your future purchases. There is a big difference between the dress code at Wimbledon in England and a tennis center in, say, New York. You probably don't want to stand out from the crowd in your choice of clothing, so investigate first.

BALLS

Try to buy any of the well-known makes of ball. When you are starting tennis they don't have to be top-of-the-range balls. But don't skimp on the number you buy, or you may spend most of your time looking for them and picking them up. Aim to have between six and twelve, all roughly of the same level of use. With young children aged about four to nine, it is advisable to purchase the special low-compression tennis balls or mini-balls, which make it easier for them to develop basic technical and tactical skills.

Clothing for tennis needs to be suitable for this physically demanding game. Don't buy your clothing for the sake of the label—buy it for your comfort. Considerations to take into account include freedom of movement, weather conditions, and dress code.

Weather

For most people, tennis is played as an outdoor game. When you play indoors you do not have to deal with the problems presented by the weather. These outdoor conditions create interesting challenges for the players and can in many ways seriously affect their level of performance. What can you do to ensure you play to your optimum in any of the weather conditions described at right?

Well, one golden rule is not to become depressed if your standard is a little below usual. Most players will play fewer "sweet" shots in adverse weather conditions.

So, if you are struggling a little, remember that your opponent will be struggling, too. The weather affects both of you equally—unless, of course, you haven't made allowances for it and your opponent has!

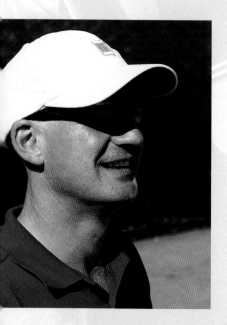

You should try to anticipate weather conditions and dress accordingly. Sunglasses and a baseball cap provide good protection against sunshine.

A FEW WEATHER TIPS

Here are a few tips to help you cope in different weather conditions.

Bright and sunny
Try to make your opponent play shots where he has to look into the sun.
- Wear a peaked cap.
- Wear sunglasses.

With the wind behind you
- Use more topspin.
- Hit more gently.
- Hit lower over the net.

With the wind against you
Hit higher over the net.
Hit harder.
Hit with less topspin.

With the wind from your right
Forehand line shot, aim toward the sideline.
Backhand line shot, aim well into the court.
Forehand crosscourt, aim well into the court.
Backhand crosscourt, aim toward the sideline.

With the wind from your left
Reverse the instructions above.

Gusty wind
Keep thinking and adapting.

Damp conditions
The balls become wetter and heavier.
Hit a little harder.
Hit higher over the net.

This is a small selection of the conditions that may affect your performance. See the weather not as a problem but as a challenge to overcome!

Etiquette

The International Tennis Federation rules and regulations are used by all the sport's national governing bodies and are usually available through clubs, tennis centers, schools, and other places where tennis is played or taught. However, there are some unwritten rules and regulations that govern court behavior. Here are some rules of tennis etiquette to keep in mind:

Tennis is a fun sport. Don't make it a war— make it a challenge.

1 When players are playing a point, do not distract them by walking behind their court.

2 Never interrupt a point for any reason (unless a safety issue has arisen).

3 When your opponent serves into the net don't call out "fault"; it is unnecessary.

4 Try not to make too much noise on your court; you may distract your opponent or even people on the next court.

5 Wear the correct footwear and clothing as advised in the club regulations.

6 Cell phones should be switched off while on court.

7 Do not continually challenge your opponent's line calls. If she is that bad at line decisions, don't bother to play with her again.

8 Always at the end of your game leave the court as clean and tidy as you would want to find it.

9 Always vacate your court two to three minutes before the end of your allocated booking time, to enable new players to begin on the hour.

10 If you are not sure of any rule or regulation, ask your playing partner. If he doesn't know, try to find out from someone who does. Don't rely on a person who seems vague or just thinks he knows.

11 If a ball lands near the line and you are not sure whether it is in or out, discuss it with your opponent and come to an agreement (possibly play it again). Never guess in your own favor—that can be seen as cheating.

12 Always be a good sport and enjoy the challenge of competition. Remember that there's no disgrace in losing. Try to reach your personal best and you will enjoy the match. Tennis is a wonderful game, so have fun!

Glossary

Approach shot a stroke that is hit deep into the opponent's court, enabling the player to move toward the net

Attack zone the area from approximately 6.5 feet (2m) inside the baseline to the service line

Backhand a return stroke that is played on the left side of a right-handed player and on the right side of a left-handed player

Baseline the lengthwise end boundary of a tennis court, running parallel to the net

Building zone the area up to 6.5 feet (2m) inside the baseline

Crosscourt shot a stroke hit diagonally from one side of the court to the other

Defense zone the area behind the baseline

Down-the-line shot a stroke that is hit straight (not diagonally) from one side of the court to the other

Drive volley a stroke with a longer swing than used for an ordinary volley

Drop shot a delicate stroke that just clears the net and then falls abruptly in the opponent's court

Forehand a right-handed player returns the ball to the right, and a left-handed player to the left

Hitting zone the area 2 feet (0.6m) before contact with the ball and 2 feet (0.6m) after contact

Kick serve a serve hit with heavy topspin, which makes the ball bounce higher and to the right

Lob the ball is hit high into the air, over the opponent's head, toward the back of the court

Passing shot a shot that is hit down the line past an opponent at the net

Service line a line joining the sidelines of a tennis court, parallel to the net

Short ball a misplayed ball that allows an opportunity to attack

Slice the ball is hit with backspin and lower over the net than normal, so that it generally bounces lower

Smash a powerful overhead stroke often used to return an unsuccessful lob

Split step the player jumps slightly, pushing against the ground on landing, and is then ready for a quick start

Target area a small area in the opponent's service box to which the server directs the racket face

Topspin the ball is hit with a brushing action, altering the trajectory of its flight and allowing a greater margin for error in clearing the net

Unforced errors the player makes mistakes without being forced into them by the opponent

Volley the ball is hit before it bounces, mostly when the player is close to the net

Index

Index

Credits

Quarto and the author would like to thank and
acknowledge Sarah Kirby, Lesley Jones, Steve Pike,
James Wellings, and Pete Harris for giving up their time to
model for the photography.
Quarto and the author would also like to thank and
acknowledge David Lloyd Leisure (Cheshire Oaks),
Ellesmere Port, South Wirral for allowing us to use their
premises for photography purposes.